91

AF208048

Succeeding in
Corporate America

Succeeding in Corporate America

A Case Study of a Black American against the Odds

William R. Spivey, Ph.D.

VANTAGE PRESS
New York

FIRST EDITION

All rights reserved, including the right of
reproduction in whole or in part in any form.

Copyright © 1991 by William R. Spivey, Ph.D.

Published by Vantage Press, Inc.
516 West 34th Street, New York, New York 10001

Manufactured in the United States of America
ISBN: 0-533-09488-7

Library of Congress Catalog Card No.: 90-90497

1 2 3 4 5 6 7 8 9 0

This book is designed to be used as a learning aid for work force diversity training and guidance for minority and female employees.

This book is dedicated
to Tanya, Aba, and Sandra
the loves of my life—

NO ONE IS AN ISLAND

No one is an island, everyone needs to be wanted.
To be wanted, you must be known;
To be known, you must build relationships;
To build relationships, you must communicate;
To communicate, you must have something to say;
To have something to say, you must have a plan;
To have a plan, you must know where you are going;
To know where you are going, you must know where you are;
To know where you are, you must know who you are;
To know who you are is the beginning.

—William R. Spivey, 1990

Contents

Foreword

It is rare to find an autobiographic study like this one. Dr. Spivey's book is a delight as imaginative literature enjoyable to read and as a display with larger implications for studies of human development, interactive social sciences, and the applied sciences of management, administration, education, and urban affairs. In the study he places himself, a modern executive, in the context of the long history of the events surrounding race in American economics and society. He fills the story with punch lines, directed toward ambitious Black members of the U.S. work force and their families, America's most important minority. Meanwhile, the reader who is White will be as enthralled by this story, since all are part of the drama Dr. Spivey brings to these pages.

    The author is a Black scientist who has risen in business. He did not get derailed, in spite of many disadvantages. His first concern is with societal life in the United States. Then he shows—with that special imaginative drama that only an introspective life story can show—the distortions in corporate settings as they really occur and as they accumulate into "Corporate Drag," with its avoidable financial consequences. In writing this book, the author's purpose was to throw light on a large research project of his about Black and White professionals in Corporate America. He decided to conduct an introspective study of himself while conducting a large study of others, to illuminate the important factors in both perspectives. For the individual, this method of introspective study is a fine example. Dr. Spivey describes here his "lessons" and converts them into what I will call definitive guidelines. For this reason the book can serve as a learning tool for groups, to use in ways similar to the author's own purpose. (I use it as a text in an adult course offered in a high-technology industrial community in Minnesota.)

I find the author to be a real harbinger on a frontier that is just beginning to dawn on the American consciousness. The frontier is caused by our Affirmative Action gains. We begin to perceive our great losses, by which we continue to suffer in the grip of exclusionary thinking in the United States. We know we lose because we carry still a history of stated intentions to turn that around. From Dr. Spivey's particular style as an interdisciplinarian, between physics and the organizational sciences and the art of a storyteller, much of what one will derive from this book is intuitive. That vital aspect, the intuitive product, is an effect felt by the reader beyond the logical or analytic aspects of his words. We have here a story of human control among groups, told by an ambitious man who would, and did, elevate his career against the odds. Here he will explain how. . . .

PROFESSOR MARGARET B. MILLER-VAUGHAN
St. Cloud, 1991

Preface

Although it is widely known that the American work force is increasing in its diversity, few companies have recognized the different managerial training and skill-building required. The work force is no longer a uniform body but includes a wide variety of knowledge workers. Women, Blacks, Hispanics, and others are becoming an ever increasing percentage of the employee population. Diversity brings with it a new set of issues for the White male manager and leaders of the future. Work force diversity is to White male business leaders what the iceberg was to the captain of the Titanic when he ordered full steam ahead. He found most of his issues were below the surface.

The changing ratio of Blacks to Whites in Corporate America, history has shown, will lead to increased racial tension. The problem identified here is the difference in managerial behaviors caused by racial assumptions that are neither substantiable nor work-related. The practice of racism, it is believed, will continue to plague Corporate America's progress. This remains one of Corporate America's biggest dilemmas. The changing demographics will continue to exacerbate the dilemma and force solutions. The solutions will not be cost-free in the short run, but gains will be great in the longer run.

This is a case study of WRS, a Black American male, and the trials and tribulations he experienced during his quest toward becoming a successful professional in America. A key question is addressed. How does a Black deal with racism when it appears in his path to success? To be sure, success is in the eyes of the beholder. In the context used here, it is taken to mean rising to a position of significant responsibility and influence in Corporate America. This book segments the significant periods of the case study as follows: "The Early Years (1951–1957)," "Self-Preparation (1958–1969)," and finally, "Corporate America, Part I (1970–1978)" and "Corporate America, Part II (1978–1990)." The final chapters summarize the important lessons learned for readers who desire to use this case study as a model for developing their corporate strategy. Also included is a discussion of the implications of the growing number of Blacks in the work environment of Corporate America. This case study forms the basis for the implications. The conclusion reached is that evidence exists that racism did and will continue to influence the success of Black professionals along their journey in Corporate America.

Succeeding in Corporate America

Chapter 1

Introduction

The nature of the subject matter has its origin in history. Blacks have struggled through slavery and continue to encounter prejudice and discrimination while assimilating into society. The increased growth in population and persistence in their 300-year plight have contributed to an increase in number within the corporate environment where the struggle continues. Many authors would suggest that the different attributes Blacks bring to the corporate setting explain why Whites employ discrimination. Blacks are realizing that prejudice and discrimination are just as prevalent in the corporate setting as they are in society as a whole. What are the challenges Blacks face in the work environment? What forces, if any, are at work against them? Will the experience of discrimination be encountered within Corporate America? Numerous writers have written about the Black professional's experience in the corporate environment, and believed they found racism. (See Appendix A.)

By the time Blacks enter the work environment, the experience of racial prejudice and discrimination has developed deep roots within their personality. This makes it difficult for trust-building managerial practices to take hold. Trust building in the Corporate Setting between Blacks and

Whites is not a natural process. The Corporate environment becomes a collective drama where actors role-play and maneuver through the workday. Unfortunately, as in the larger society, most of the burden of change actually rests with the victim.

This is a case study of WRS, a Black American male, and the trials and tribulations he experienced during his quest toward becoming a successful professional in America. He was, as all Americans both Black and White, a product of his environment. He was born in 1946 in Brunswick, Georgia, during a time of high racial tension resulting from the segregation, the hatred, and the prejudice which existed between Whites and Blacks. His values were influenced and shaped by the harsh reality of racism. Unquestionably it was a hostile environment. How does a Black deal with racism when it blocks his path to success?

To be sure, success is in the eyes of the beholder. In the context used here, it is taken to mean rising to a position of significant responsibility and influence in Corporate America. As the number of Blacks increases and they become more educated, history has shown that an increase in resistance toward them will occur within the White majority. To be sure, rising to a vice presidential level in Corporate America is a significant accomplishment for anyone, White or Black. For a Black to accomplish this during the period between 1970 and 1990 was a very difficult task.

This is a chronicle of challenges and activities across the life of a Black executive in two of America's most historic corporations. America would like to be viewed as a country that stands for justice, dignity, equality, and freedom for all of its citizens. In this chronicle, as elsewhere, there is clear evidence that America's adoption of principles and the uniform implementation of them are separate challenges. The attitudes of White America about equality for non-

Whites are clearly reflected in people's behavior. Eitzen and Baca-Zinn (1989) state:

> . . . racial and ethnic stratification is the basic feature of American society. It is built into society's policies and practices that may appear neutral but systematically exclude people on the basis of race and ethnicity, thus creating majority and minority relations (p. 202).

The minority groups are generally smaller in population, have lower economic status relative to the majority (less property, lower per capita income), less education, lower job status, they lack power and influence, and they experience prejudice and discrimination. Systematic exclusion is a form of human control.

Lerone Bennett, Jr. (1969) began his book *The Shaping of Black America* as follows:

> In August, when the shadows are long on the land and even the air oppresses, the furies of fate hang in the balance in black America. It was in August, in the eighth month of the year, that three hundred thousand men and women marched on Washington, D.C. It was in August that Watts exploded. It was in August, on a hot and heavy day in the nineteenth century, that Nat Turner rode. And it was in another August, 344 years before the march on Washington, 346 years before Watts, and 212 years before Nat Turner's war, that "a Dutch man of Warr" sailed up the river James and landed the first generation of black Americans at Jamestown, Virginia (p. 5).

Since the landing of the first generations of Blacks, America has not been the same. The enslavement of Blacks, based on the belief that they were an inferior race, started the uphill battle by Blacks for equal rights. This points to a value system for Whites that has formulated White attitudes towards Blacks that has lasted for over 300 years. Behavioral evidence of it persists in the American society today.

The United States represents a collage of different ethnic and racial groups. While all of these groups came to the United States under different circumstances, Blacks were the only ones brought against their will as slaves. America's history is rich with different views of the myths and truths about slavery and its ensuing influence on Black development. In America, the land of opportunity, equality has a different meaning for Blacks from its meaning for Whites. For Whites, equality in treatment is an inalienable right; for Blacks, it must be earned. In order to earn this right, White society has established White norms to which non-Whites adhere in order to be fully accepted into society. These norms are also impeding the progress of Blacks in society. This case study reveals how a Black American responded to this challenge and how racism influenced his development.

This book segments the significant periods of this case study as follows: The Early Years (1951–1957); The Self-Preparation (1958–1969); and finally, The Journey through Corporate America—in two parts—spanning 1970–1990. During 1951–1957, WRS attended grade school while growing up in a ghetto. During this period, he began to realize what it was like to experience discrimination. He also established a strong desire to somehow overcome the inhumane treatment he and his family were receiving. During the period 1958–1969, a growing maturity reveals the realism of his challenge. He began to crystallize the difficulty he faced in order to overcome the obstacles along his path. His education helped him obtain a more mature vision of what he needed to do and the understanding needed to begin. He became convinced that a good education, the right work experience, and careful planning were essential ingredients.

Finally, the period between 1970–1990 marked the time

when the corporate journey began and success was achieved. A journey in Corporate America is analogous to the crossing of a field of land mines without having knowledge of where the mines are located. The heightened awareness of the risk of taking an incorrect step, detrimental to success, is very keen.

The final chapters summarize the important lessons learned. The lessons should be useful to the reader who desires to use this case study as a model for a corporate strategy. Also included is a discussion of the implications for Corporate America of the growing number of Blacks in the work environment. It gives evidence that racism does now and will continue to influence the strategies of Black professionals along their journey toward success in Corporate America.

Chapter 2

The Early Years (1951-1957)

A. The Environment

Black Families

Billingsley's (1968) concept of the Black family as a social system[1] is illustrated by Figure 1.

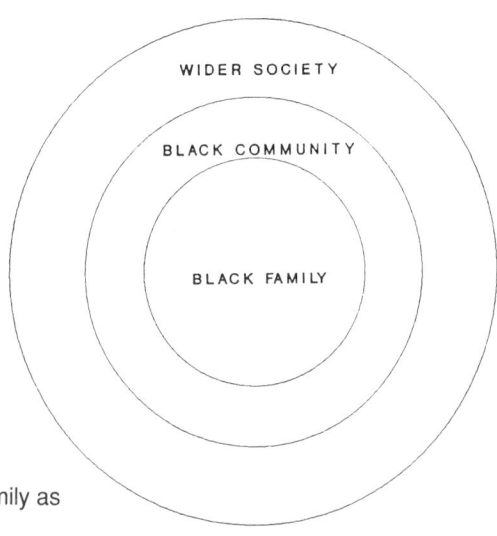

Figure 1 The Black Family as a Social System.

The Negro family is imbedded in a network of mutually interdependent relationships with the Negro community and the wider society.

The Negro family includes within itself several subsystems: that of the Husband-Wife, and those of Mother-Son, Mother-Daughter, Father-Son, Father-Daughter, Brother-Sister, Brother-Brother, Sister-Sister, and sometimes the Grandmother-Mother-Daughter subsystems, to mention only the most common.

The Negro community includes within itself a number of institutions which may also be viewed as subsystems. Prominent among these are: schools, churches, taverns, newspapers, neighborhood associations, lodges, fraternities, social clubs, age and sex peer groups, recreation associations, and small businesses, including particularly, barber shops, beauty parlors, restaurants, pool halls, funeral societies, and various organized systems of hustling.

The wider society consists of major institutions which help set the conditions for Negro family life. Chief among these are the subsystem of values, the political, economic, education, health, welfare, and communications subsystems (Billingsley 1968, p.7).

The four major concepts Billingsley provided indicate the essential elements in this perspective: (1) a social system; (2) ethnic subsociety; (3) family structure; and (4) family function. Each of these, they state, has major concepts and refer to a stream of social science theory which has been developed and tested primarily in relation to other social phenomena in the family (4). Within Billingsley's concept, where the wider society is White with different norms, there is reason to see an almost "containment" type of strategy by White society to keep Blacks within their own community. The family is at the heart of child development. The norms which are learned there (Black norms), will be carried forward into the wider society (White norms). Ethnocentrism, the belief in cultural superiority, will result in Black culture being judged inferior to White. This will result in a feeling of rejection (psychological deprivation). Billingsley (1968) states:

> It is becoming difficult for Negro parents to teach their children to hide the hate and fear way inside. The dilemmas facing the Negro parent in rearing their children in the face of these conflicting demands are deep and intricate (p. 31).

This disadvantage attributed to Black development will contribute to the difficulty for Blacks in achieving equality. Billingsley concludes:

> One implication of this point of view is that whatever ails the Negro family is a reflection of ailments in the society at large. The cure for those ills is not likely to be found in any single or simple solution . . . and successful efforts to include the Negro people into the society as equals using the same ingenuity and dedication as has been used to exclude them might benefit the whole society (p. 32).

The argument that Blacks' underachievement is due to not working as hard as Whites begins to become diluted when you look at Billingsley's family concept.

The following are a number of key milestones just prior to and during the early years of this case study. These milestones are taken from Bennett (1987):

> On January 3, 1947, NAACP issued a report which described: "one of the grimmest years in the history of the National Association for the Advancement of Colored People." The report deplored "reports of blow torch killing and eye gouging of Negro veterans freshly returned from a

war to end torture and racial extermination" and said, "Negroes in America have been disillusioned over the wave of lynchings, brutality, and official recession from all of the flamboyant promises of post war democracy and decency" (p. 541).

On October 29, 1947, the President's committee for Civil Rights condemned racial injustices in America in a formal report, "To Secure These Rights" (p. 542).

July 26, 1948, President Truman issued Executive Order Number 9981 directing, "equality of treatment and opportunity" in the Armed Forces (p. 544).

In 1950 the United States population was 150 million people, of which 10% were Black (p. 545).

On February 16, 1951, New York City Council passed a Bill prohibiting racial discrimination in city assisted housing development. On May 24, 1951, racial segregation in Washington, D.C., restaurants ruled illegal by Municipal Court of Appeals (p. 547).

On June, 1951, "NAACP began a frontal attack on segregation and discrimination in elementary and high school levels, arguing that segregation was discrimination in cases before three judge federal courts in South Carolina and Kansas. The South Carolina court, with a strong dissent from Judge E. Waites Waring, held that segregation was not discrimination, June 23. Kansas court ruled that the separate facilities at issue were equal but said that segregation had an adverse effect on Black children" (p. 547).

On July 12, 1951, Governor Adlai Stevenson called out National Guard to stop rioting in Cicero, Illinois. Mob of 3,500 tried to keep a Black family from moving into an all-White city (p. 547).

On December 30, 1952, Tuskeegee Institute reported that 1952 was the first year in 71 years of tabulation that there were no lynchings in America (p. 548).

On June 8, 1953, the U. S. Supreme Court banned

segregation in Washington, D.C., restaurants (p. 548).

On August 4, 1953, movement of Black families into Trumbel Park Housing Park in Chicago triggered virtually continuous riots which lasted more than three years and required assignment of more than 1,000 policemen to keep order (p. 549).

On May 17, 1954, the U.S. Supreme Court in the landmark Brown vs. Board of Education decision declared segregation of public schools unconstitutional. The unanimous decision was read by Chief Justice Earl B. Warren (p. 549).

On May 31, 1955, the Supreme Court ordered school integration "with all deliberate speed" (p. 551).

On Dec. 1, 1955, Rosa Parks, a seamstress and activist was arrested after she refused to give her seat to a White man on a Montgomery, Alabama, bus (p. 551).

On January 30, 1956, home of Martin Luther King, Jr., Montgomery bus boycott leader, bombed (p. 552).

On April 23, 1956, the U.S. Supreme Court refused to review lower court decision which banned segregation in intrastate bus travel (p. 557).

On June 5, 1956, federal court ruled that racial segregation on Montgomery city buses violated constitution (p. 552).

On September 12, 1956, Black students entered Clay, Kentucky, Elementary School under National Guard protection. They were barred from the school on September 17 (p. 552).

On November 13, 1956, the Supreme Court upheld lower court decision which banned segregation on city buses in Montgomery, Alabama. Federal injunctions prohibiting segregation on the buses were served on city, state, and bus company officials December 20. At two mass meetings, Montgomery Blacks called off year-long bus boycott. Buses were integrated on December 21.

On August 29, 1957, Congress passed the Civil Rights

Act of 1957, the first federal civil rights legislation since 1875. The bill established a Civil Rights Commission and a civil rights division in the Justice Department and also gave the Justice Department authority to seek injunctions against voting rights infractions. On September 9, Nashville's new Hattie Cotton Elementary School with enrollment of 1 Black and 388 Whites virtually destroyed by a dynamite blast and also during that same month, Rev. F. L. Shuttleworth mobbed when he attempted to enroll his daughters in "White" Birmingham school (p. 554).

On September 24, 1957, President Eisenhower ordered federal troops to Little Rock, Arkansas to prevent interference with school integration at Central High School (p. 554).

There is clear indication that Blacks, although created equal, are not exposed to the same environmental conditions which are needed to expose them to an equal opportunity of achievement in the wider society. Montagu (1975) states:

> ... in the case of Blacks and Whites, because Blacks have never enjoyed equal cultural and social economic opportunities in any White society, Blacks in America have, in fact, been deprived, oppressed, discriminated against, impoverished, and ghettoized, and generally excluded from the brotherhood of man. Hence, it should not be surprising that there has been and continues to be significant difference in the achievements of Blacks and Whites as measured by tests which have been arbitrarily standardized on middle class Whites (p. 3).

The uphill battle to overcome prejudice and discrimination continues to impede the Black achievement.

B. Growing Up Black in America

WRS was born on November 8, 1946. This was the day on which WRS joined the fight for freedom, a freedom of equality among equals, and to endure battle to demonstrate that he was just as capable as any other human being. Growing up Black in America is a unique experience. During one's adolescent years, one initially assumes a state of equality and then, as one grows older, one begins to realize how different one is. WRS was born as an illegitimate child in a farmhouse in the middle of a cornfield. He lived in a single-parent household. Since he had left the area with his mother at birth, they both had returned to visit the farmhouse when he was seven years old. He can remember the slum environment in which his birthplace was located. That visit was an experience he would never forget.

In the Deep South, which was the heart of the most intense Black struggle, racism grew into hate. The hate Whites had for Blacks was so intense that the White majority enforced segregationist policies. A separate and unequal society was established. All public places were divided for Blacks only and for Whites only. Blacks were forced to sit in the rear of buses or trains. In cases where the bus or train was crowded, if Blacks were sitting they had to give up their seats to Whites. Whenever Whites referred to a Black, they typically used the term "nigger." Blacks in America, and especially in the South, were experiencing a great deal of fear and intimidation. The environment, as indicated earlier, was degrading. Blacks were experiencing so much discrimination they began to rebel.

WRS grew up in this environment and as a child he was not able to play with White children. He and other Blacks were "kept" in their place. Blacks were powerless and economically deprived. Discrimination, prejudice, and racism were rampant in the South. Like many Black families, his mother decided to move north (to Pittsburgh) to seek employment and escape the pervasive violence of the South. Being very poor, they had difficulty finding an apartment which was affordable. Many Blacks who moved to the North did not have money or jobs once they arrived. The choice of affordable housing was also limited. Generally, Blacks were located in very poor neighborhoods. WRS remembers the insect infestation in his apartment. He and his mother shared a community bathroom with other tenants on the floor. The convenience of a private bathroom was a luxury that they could not afford.

WRS's first year of school was 1951. During his school years, 1951–1957, WRS began to understand what it was like to be Black in America. Blacks were viewed and treated as inferior to Whites. He had one friend (Bobby) who was White. Although Bobby's family lived next door, they were quite prosperous. Their house was very different in its internal richness and quality. Bobby's parents owned a tavern which was located in the lower level of their house. WRS and Bobby played in the alleyway between the two houses. Although they grew up together, Bobby attended an all-White school in a different neighborhood. They were allowed to play together frequently in spite of the racial tension in their neighborhood. The contrast in the two life-styles of their families left a lasting impression on WRS. The important distinction between the two life-styles was a matter of family income.

The North was very different from the South. Blacks were able to use the same public facilities as Whites. WRS remembered this as being very odd and could not clearly understand the difference geography made. Many Blacks living in the North were transplants from the South. They had moved North to seek jobs, a better living, and also to avoid the intense racism which existed in the South. The jobs which Blacks were able to obtain were mostly manual labor. WRS's mother was able to acquire employment in a shirt laundry. Her job was typical of the type of job many Southern Blacks were able to acquire. She, like many Blacks, had to quit school at an early age in order to support herself and her parents.

Other aspects of WRS's childhood were "normal." He played in Little League baseball, which became his most active school sport. Considering the amount of racial unrest, he was able to balance his time between school and sports while staying out of trouble. WRS remembers that his mother was very proud of his achievements. She taught him how to survive with little and to find satisfaction with what he had. Although these were very lean years (with very little money, space, or food), and discrimination existed in the North, it was an improvement over the deep-seated overt racism that existed in the South.

NOTE

1. A system is an organization of units or elements united in some form of regular interaction and interdependence . . . the key words in this definition are units, organization, interaction, and interdependence . . . a social system is an aggregation of persons or social roles bound together in a pattern of mutual interaction and interdependence (Billingsley [1968] p. 4).

Chapter 3

Self-Preparation (1958-1969)

A. The Environment

Introduction

The following identifies very significant activities which occurred during WRS's high school and college years. Dr. King's non-violent leadership and Stokeley Carmichael's more radical approach had a profound influence on WRS's beliefs.

These leaders helped create an environment in which he was a part. He actively engaged in the marches, sit-ins, and was a recipient of the violence which occurred.

Dr. King's Era

Dr. Martin Luther King, Jr. was the most influential civil rights leader of our time. His approach was to appeal to the moral conscience of White America. Dr. King stated in his letter from Birmingham Jail that no help would come from anyone

> . . . who paternalistically believes he can set the timetable for another man's freedom; who lives by a mythical concept of

time and who constantly advises the Negro to wait for a "more convenient season." Shallow understanding from people of good will is more frustrating than absolute misunderstanding from people of ill will. Lukewarm acceptance is much more bewildering than outright rejection (Schulke [1976], p. 216).

Changes in racial attitudes and behaviors have proven to be a slow process. If changes were not gradual, they were viewed as a threat against the majority norm and consequently the majority rejected them. Dr. Martin Luther King, Jr., knew it would take a long time to bring about a change from racial inequality using a non-violent approach. In his speech, "I Have a Dream," Dr. King stated:

But 100 years later, the Negro still is not free; 100 years later, the life of the Negro is still sadly crippled by the manacles of segregation and the chains of discrimination; 100 years later, the Negro lives on a lonely island of poverty in the midst of a vast ocean of material prosperity; 100 years later, the Negro still languishes in the corners of American society and finds himself in exile in his own land (Schulke [1976], p. 218).

The inner conscience of Whites needed to be tapped first. Over time Dr. King's non-violent approach was effective and slowly influenced changes in Civil Rights legislation. Whites' moral consciousness began to respond to the American creed and began relinquishing some control without giving up power. Non-Whites viewed this as progress, but it was not fast enough. As a result of the slow rate of change in civil rights policies, an escalation occurred in racial tension. Many Blacks began to look for new leadership.

The slow rate of change in Blacks' struggle for equality gave rise to the Stokeley Carmichael "Black Power" push. Black Power was a major interruption to King's leadership. During the struggle for Black equality, Stokeley Carmichael emerged as a radical leader pushing for Black power. His approach was radical in that it advocated violent action and an overthrowing of the White power structure. Carmichael proclaimed: "Power is the only thing respected in this world and we must get it at any cost." The slogan "Black Power" projected anger and violence toward overcoming the injustices that were taking place. The period of "Black Power" recognition had significant influence on the Black population. It made Blacks proud to be Black.

Blacks began to identify with their cultural heritage and began to look at themselves as beautiful human beings ("Black is Beautiful"). This began an era of high self-awareness and self-esteem on the part of the Black population. Sitkoff (1981) stated: "In whatever form it took, pride in being Black proved invaluable in aiding Blacks to discard the disabling self-hatred, inculcated by White culture" (p. 216). History surrounding the era of Black power will remain in controversy as to whether it helped or delayed Black progress. On the one hand, it created self-awareness and unity among the Black people, and on the other it instilled a sense of fear on the part of the majority population that Blacks were going to rise up and take over the world. This caused a decrease in the support from Whites for the Black movement toward equality. Sitkoff (1981) states: "The anti-White connotations of Black power had cooled the ardor of White liberals for the struggle" (p. 222).

Carmichael represented those who were impatient with King's approach and wanted a revolutionary change. They began to be intolerant of the non-violent approach which was, in their view, illogical. These radical leaders took literally the American creed of all men being created equal, and equality and justice for all, and wanted America to move faster or suffer the consequences of retaliation by the Black population. The plan to bring about revolutionary change and the balance of power in America (between Whites and Blacks), resulted in death and destruction. Without power and control, minorities who retaliated (through riots) against the majority failed.

Black Power was only a slogan with a meaning that varied even among the Black population. Moreover, the interpretation by the Majority population was based primarily on concern for threats against their majority control. This violent approach was suppressed through the strength and power of the Majority. This violent period slowed the progression of the evolutionary, non-violent movement of Dr. Martin Luther King, Jr. Dr. King's struggle for equality began to shift emphasis. As Wilhelm (1979) observed:

> King became one of the very first to realize that equality impedes Black opportunity; to invoke standards for judgment regardless of color introduces direct competition at just the moment when Blacks are the least able to compete. Increased poverty, poor education, deteriorating housing, higher unemployment relative to Whites are conditions that reflect and determine the lack of social resources among Blacks to compete regardless of color (p. 6).

Without economic gains, the Black population would not only suffer racism, but would be faced with impoverished living conditions. Dr. King favored an improvement in the economics of the underclass as his priority. Wilhelm (1979) states:

> The extent to which King set aside racism in favor of economics is most clearly revealed in his solution for Black survival; he called for a guaranteed income. Yet, no amount of economic subsidy will dispense with racism. Racism can and in America will flourish in spite of King's new economics; however true it may be that "Negro programs go beyond rights," White America itself remains as racist as ever without compromise. As long as the argument is made that racism is a mere product of economic conditions, then racism itself will not be eliminated. King did not set forth any particular relationship between racism and economics: he failed to inform us how these two variables intersect in a causal sense (p. 11).

This review of the Black Power push by King, Carmichael, and others can be augmented by the following summary of key milestones during the self-preparation years of this case study. These milestones are taken from Bennett (1987):

> The 1960 census had counted 179 million Americans in the U.S. and a Black population of 10.5% (p. 557).
> On April 19, 1960, the home of Z. Alexander Looby, counsel for 153 students arrested in sit-in demonstrations, destroyed by dynamite bomb. More than 2,000 students marched on the Nashville City Hall in protest (p. 558).
> On Dec. 15, 1961, police used tear gas and leashed dogs to stop mass demonstration by 1,500 Blacks in Baton Rouge, LA (p. 563).
> On Feb. 2, 1962, four Black mothers arrested after sit-in at Chicago Elementary School. Mothers later received suspended $50.00 fines. Protests, picketing, and dem-

onstrations continue for several weeks against *de facto* segregation, double shifts, and mobile classrooms (p. 564).

On Sept. 13, 1962, Mississippi Governor Ross R. Barnett defied the federal government in impassioned speech on state-wide radio/television hookup saying he would "interpose" the authority of the state between the University of Mississippi and federal judges who had ordered the admission of James H. Meredith. Barnett said, "there is no case in history where the Caucasian race has survived social integration." He promised to go to jail if necessary to prevent integration at the State University. His defiance set the stage for the gravest federal/state crisis since the Civil War (p. 566).

On Sept. 28, 1962, Governor Barnett found guilty of civil contempt of the federal court. The United States Court of Appeals for the Fifth Circuit ordered Barnett to purge himself of contempt or face arrest and a fine of $10,000 a day (p. 567).

On November 20, 1962, President Kennedy issued Executive Order barring racial discrimination in federally financed housing (p. 568).

In June 1963, President Kennedy told nation in radio/tv address that segregation was morally wrong and that it was "time to act in the Congress, in your state and local legislative body, and. . .in all of our daily lives" (p. 569).

On June 12, 1963, Medgar W. Evers, 37, NAACP Field Secretary in Mississippi, assassinated in front of his Jackson home by a segregationist (p. 569).

On August 28, 1963, more than 250,000 persons participated in March on Washington demonstration, the largest civil rights demonstration in history (p. 569).

Sept. 15, 1963, four Black girls killed in bombing of 16th Street Baptist Church in Birmingham (p. 569).

On May 12, 1970, the race riot in Augusta, GA. Six Blacks were killed, authorities said five of the victims were shot by police (p. 588).

On Feb. 29, 1968, the National Advisory Commission on Civil Disorders (a Turner Commission) said White racism was the fundamental cause of the riots in American cities. The commission said America was "moving toward two societies, one Black, one White—separate and unequal" (p. 581).

Key legislative changes were made during this period, such as the Civil Rights Act 1964 (integration of public establishments, barring of discrimination by employers, among other things), and the Voting Rights Act 1965 (elimination of discrimination in voting, and so forth). The struggle to be treated as equals and to remove bias from decisions involving Blacks cost many lives.

In spite of all the effort put forth by many leaders for equality, the hatred continued. The end of a great era occurred as a result of the following:

On April 4, 1968, Martin Luther King, Jr., assassinated by White sniper in Memphis, TN. Assassination precipitated national crisis and rioting in more than 100 cities. Forty-six persons were killed and major rebellions in Washington, Chicago, and other cities. . .President Lyndon B. Johnson declared Sunday, April 6, a national day of mourning and ordered all U.S. flags on government buildings and all U.S. territories and possessions to fly at half-mast. (Bennett [1987], p. 581.)

Blacks had shown continued endurance for over 300 years. Without economic power or influence, and with only the appeal to the moralism of the broader White society, the chances of bringing about radical change seem to have been slim. Racism in society does make a difference in Black attainment. The power of the majority, the prejudice and discrimination which ensues, the lack of economic balance, and the inability to bring about radical change continued to play a significant role in the values, beliefs, attitudes, and behavior of the Black American. WRS is just one case.

B. Education: The Key to Success

King's Influence

Dr. King was a role model for many Blacks, WRS included. Dr. King ascended to a leadership position during a time when unity and an alternative to violence were badly needed. His non-violent religious approach had a profound effect on many of the young students. Dr. King's philosophy taught WRS alternative approaches to direct confrontation. Dr. King demonstrated excellent political skills. He knew that the inner conscience of Whites had to be reached prior to changing majority behavior. Changing behavior, he acknowledged, would take time. In order to bring about change, he exposed the inhuman side of racism to the moral majority. He created a vision and he was successful in convincing others to believe in that vision. He did extensive networking with the moral majority and developed a strong constituency. This ultimately built the momentum that was needed to successfully influence the passing of the Civil Rights Act of 1964 and the Voting Rights Act of 1965. His leadership of passive resistance during the impressionable years of WRS made an impact which he remembered. Dr. King's philosophy formulated part of the basis for WRS's philosophy and his subsequent successful strategy.

High School

WRS attended Fifth Avenue High School in Pittsburgh, Pennsylvania. This was a school which provided education for children grades 7 through 12. It was racially mixed, although 75%–80% of the students were Black. The school was in a slum area, but the facilities were above average when compared to other predominantly Black schools. It was located only a couple of miles from where he lived. Going to high school during very turbulent years, described above, made a very deep impression on the young students. As they studied history, they were also living history. Much of the external violence which occurred was brought into the classroom and into the homes. Survival was an intricate part of WRS's and other Blacks' development. As the many communities were racially separated in their feelings about equality, so were the students. This was a period of difficulty and confusion for both parents and teachers not to have as much influence as what was happening in society. WRS and other students were preoccupied with what was going on outside the class. During the early 1960s, as indicated in some of the milestones, many Black and White students alike instigated and participated in riots.

The high school years were very concentrated years. WRS believed in the value of an education and concentrated his efforts on mathematics and the sciences. The certificate of merit on page 24 (Figure 2) is very typical of what he was awarded year after year:

With many honor rolls and achievement certificates to his credit, he was awarded a four-year scholarship grant for 75% of his college tuition.

Jobs Held During School

WRS learned good work habits early in life. He had taken various jobs throughout his school years, which included: (1) a paper route; (2) shining shoes; (3) baker's helper; (4) professional billiard player; (5) parking lot attendant; and (6) tutor in mathematics. He learned how to support

FIFTH AVENUE HIGH SCHOOL

PITTSBURG PUBLIC SCHOOLS

Superintendent

Certificate of Merit

This Certificate is Granted to

WILLIAM SPIVEY

FOR EXCELLENT ACHIEVEMENT IN SCHOLARSHIP AND CITIZENSHIP

March 19, 1959

Date

_____ Principal _____ Teacher

Figure 2 A Certificate of Merit Given to WRS for Scholastic Achievement.

himself, and found that nothing came easy. Since no one was pushing him to achieve goals, he became a self-starter. He learned that if he did not take the initiative, he would become involved, through peer pressure, as either part of a gang or on drugs.

First Mentor

In spite of the initiative and drive he had, WRS learned that one cannot succeed without the help of others. His history teacher developed his interest, realized his potential, and began to work with him. Later in high school, she became his first mentor. When WRS was trying to decide between college and the Armed Services, she provided him counseling. She assisted him in obtaining a scholarship (mentioned earlier) and encouraged him to attend college. She was very sincere in her efforts. He began to focus his energy on education and did whatever he could to make her proud of him. This was a truly pivotal point in his life. Without the help of his history teacher at a very important time, the outcome might have been different.

College

Attending college was a very stressful experience, much more than high school. In addition to the academic challenge and the new environment, he also had a full-time job. WRS attended Duquesne University in Pittsburgh, Pennsylvania, during a time when the University had a student body of 10,000 students, with only 8 Blacks. His major area of study was in the physical sciences while pursuing a degree in Physics.

During WRS's undergraduate studies, his attitude about his environment was that of most college students during this period, all-knowing and rebellious against the Vietnam War. Blacks were also fighting for equality. There was a high degree of racial tension as riots continued in the South and began to start up in the North. There were many occasions when martial law had to be imposed. He was actively involved in the struggle for Black equality which added to the difficulty of adjusting to college life. He had difficulty balancing his social environment with the demand of his academic studies. He realized late in his college career that a serious commitment to education was a long-range process and he became serious about the need for academic excellence.

Unlike many of his classmates, he was fortunate not to have been drafted into the Vietnam War. This close call with the draft influenced his attitude toward education.. At the time, majoring in Physics while maintaining good grades somehow had an influence in the selection process. Education began to be viewed as the key to success. He later graduated in 1968.

Graduate School

By the time he had been accepted into graduate school, the need for education had really caught on. It became very evident that education played a significant role in achieving success and, he hoped, racial equality. In order to have Black Power, contrary to what Stokeley Carmichael had advocated, you needed "knowledge power." Education might have been the best weapon Blacks had during this period. Knowledge power became almost an obsession to WRS. With a high degree of concentration during his graduate studies, he was able to complete the Masters program at Indiana University, Indiana, Pennsylvania, within a year. He graduated in 1969 with a Master of Science Degree in Physics specializing in low energy nuclear physics. He then pursued additional graduate studies at Bryn Mawr College, Bryn Mawr, Pennsylvania.

WRS knew that the pursuit of further specialization in the area of nuclear physics at the Ph.D. level required an unwavering commitment to study, a high degree of maturity, time management, as well as other sacrifices. In spite of this, he got married and began a family concurrent with attending school. These changes added a degree of complexity which was not anticipated. Furthermore, due to a cutback in government funding for nuclear research, his dissertation project was delayed beyond the time objective he could financially afford. It became very difficult for him to balance his graduate studies with family and financial requirements. He decided to leave the academic environment to pursue a career in Corporate America.

Chapter 4

Corporate America, Part I (1970–1978)

A. The Environment

Facilitated by government requirements (Equal Employment Opportunity Act, July 2, 1964), higher education among Blacks, and changing demographics, the composition of Corporate America's work force began to change. Changes in ethnicity began to lead to new and different expectations of the employee populations. For many years the changing distribution of the social environment had caused some social reform. Corporations still had to reform. During the 1960s and 1970s, the government's EEO policies were beginning to have an influence. These policies began to accelerate the acceptance of Blacks in the work force. Despite historic appeals, the racial discrimination evident prior to 1970 of White against Black remained ingrained in the basic values, attitudes, and behaviors of Whites for the twenty-year period (1970–1990).

Schuman, Steeh, and Bobo (1985) did an analysis of data taken in a survey over time (1942–1984) by Gallup, National Opinion Research Center (NORC), and the Institute for Social Research (ISR), of the racial attitudes that existed in America. They noted that racial beliefs and opinions characteristic of Whites in the 40s established an atmosphere in which racism and discrimination could flourish with little challenge. Conflicts arising out of the social communities reflected in the work environment. White racism and lack of trust or understanding among Blacks and Whites had slowed Black acceptance in White society; similar factors were slowing their progress in Corporate America.

The roots of cynicism and mistrust are monitored in three studies. Schuman, Steeh, and Bobo (1985) observed that the dominant belief is that Blacks deserve the same treatment and respect as Whites (p. 202). They observed that both Blacks and Whites were less likely to endorse implementation than the principles themselves, pointing out that the gap is not nearly as wide for Blacks as for Whites. They concluded: "The fact that Whites are much less likely to support concrete implementation of principles than principles themselves, testifies to conflicts over the extent and type of possible integration" (p. 205). Campbell (1971) states:

> The one general characteristic of the White population which is dramatically related to racial orientation is college education. The educational system our respondents passed through had relatively little impact on their attitudes regarding race if they went no further than high school graduation (p. 157).

Racism was not as obvious in the more educated, perhaps due to better communication skills and more subtle pronouncements of their feelings. This was also the experience WRS encountered in Corporate America, discussed below. Wilson (1978) argues that there is a declining significance of race and that the relative economic position of Blacks in society is a more important problem than racial discrimination. However, he concludes: ". . . the mere fact of seeing Blacks in certain jobs might have been enough to generate concern among some Whites who felt that Blacks should be "kept in their place' " (p. 84).

During this period, Dickens and Dickens (1982) did a study on the Black manager in the corporate world consisting of a number of interviews with Black professionals. They state:

> Corporations and other institutions represent a microcosm of our larger society. Racism pervades every walk of our lives and presents barriers to success for that minority person in addition to whatever his or her individual shortcomings may be. For that reason, the minority managers must acquire additional coping behaviors over others and those acquired by managers in general. Also, many Black managers feel they bring some cultural differences to the White organization that may enhance or hamper their development and successes (p. x).

They concluded: "There tends to be a lack of trust on the part of the Black individual toward the White resource and an inability to sense and properly react to racism" (p. 140). They also observed that there seem to be radically different perceptions between Blacks and Whites. Blacks, they observed, appeared to behave in a friendly manner with Whites because it was felt this would allow for them to function better in the corporate setting. This friendly behavior, they concluded, was strategically important in order to become a part of the *network*. Some Whites felt they had been fair because they had treated Blacks the same as Whites. They also observed that some White male managers would tell Blacks that they are different from other Blacks in order to influence their behavior and to elevate their own comfort zone in their relationships to Blacks. Each of these observations carried separate interpretations, White or Black, and point to persistent inappropriate human control.

In any case, a common conclusion to the above reports on race relations in the United States during this case study is that, although there has been significant progress made over the last 300 years, White American values still included racism which knowingly or unknowingly shaped the attitude and behavior of the White/Black interaction. Little is known about how racism influences decision-making relative to White/Black interactions in the work environment. The following are actual incidences that happened in WRS's case during Part I of his Corporate Period.

B. Starting Out

The beginning of WRS's career was very intimidating. He had a very naïve understanding of what was involved.

His first job was obtained through a "career weekend," where companies interviewed prospective employees during a weekend. His initial job hunt proved successful. He was offered a job as a nuclear engineer at General Electric's semiconductor division. His first job assignment was a perfect choice. It allowed him to use his specialized knowledge in nuclear physics.

WRS's first job assignment lasted approximately six months. Cutbacks in government funding that had affected his doctoral research also affected the project to which he was assigned. This led to his layoff. This event had a devastating impact on his sense of job security. Job security was not guaranteed. In Corporate America, you were a contingent resource. One's first priority, WRS came to understand, was to one's self. This was an important first and significant lesson in his experience in the corporate environment. This, he later learned, was an important guiding force to human behavior within organizations. Having lost his job presented

WRS with an important dilemma. There were no other assignments which required his expertise since his expertise was in nuclear physics. To continue in his field, he would have to relocate. His former manager offered him an alternative that required him to change his field of interest to solid state physics. After a brief, unsuccessful search for a job in the nuclear field, he accepted his former manager's offer. He became a semiconductor engineer. As a semiconductor engineer, he began designing different electronic circuitry to be used in various sensor products. Taking this offer proved to be a wise choice because it involved a newly emerging technology.

After the first year of research, WRS presented a paper to his colleagues on his research findings. The research paper was on the subject of temperature sensoring technology. He had made new discoveries about design, material choices, and product performance criteria using new innovative techniques. Shortly into the presentation, he found himself being challenged very intensely by an all-White peer group of scientists. The intensity and the type of questions which were being asked did not seem to have been caused by the material being presented. The audience's focus appeared to be heavily charged on discrediting the results of the research findings. WRS had been put on the defensive. He found himself defending his credibility, understanding, and the accuracy of the research. This, he believed, was his first encounter with a professional (or personal) attack. He was the only Black engineer in the division. He had to adjust to the work environment (the change from academics to corporate life) while working with only White professionals. This experience proved to be very educational, and it modified his belief that personal performance evaluations were based solely on the results produced. This, he believed, was his first encounter with overt racial bias in the work environment.

WRS's manager had been in the audience while he was presenting his paper. He later asked his manager what his reaction to the audience's questions was. His manager had been aware that certain members in the audience had not approved of him hiring a Black. He also pointed out that since there were few Blacks in the division, many of the engineers did not have any experience working with Blacks. In addition, many of the professionals had limited exposure to Blacks outside their work environment. WRS's manager told him because of this he should prepare himself to expect a certain amount of bias toward his work. His manager's feedback proved to be very valuable in the understanding of his work environment. WRS's reaction to peer bias toward his work had to be managed. The lesson was very valuable.

WRS concluded that establishing his personal credibility would have to be a prerequisite to obtaining credibility for his work. Although this applied to both White and Black professionals, Blacks had to overcome the belief that their performance was inferior to their White peers. WRS was fortunate to have learned this early in his career. He also found it helpful to have reported to a manager who was sensitive to his dilemma.

The lesson learned during his first job assignment was an important lesson toward understanding human behavior, specifically Whites' behavior toward Blacks. To know his subject was not enough. He had to know his audience in order to develop the right communication strategy. He found that whenever he was communicating to an all-White audience, he had to establish personal credibility so that the focus of attention was not on him but on the material that was being presented.

C. Obtaining the First Managerial Assignment

Fernandez (1975) did a comprehensive study of Black managers in White corporations worldwide. One of the primary purposes of his investigation was to demonstrate an immediate need for concrete determinate action by government, business, and society in general to improve the situation for Black managers in the predominately White business world. His research provided a very comprehensive analysis of Blacks' circumstances within the corporate setting. A sample group of 272 managers, 156 White and 116 Blacks, was studied.

One of the reasons why Fernandez's study was significant was that prior to 1975 it was believed that there were not enough Black managers in the business world to conduct a meaningful study. In addition, there was clear evidence that Blacks were excluded from management; however, questions were rarely asked about the racial composition of managerial ranks. Of the eight firms studied, six are listed in Fortune 500. He used an eight-part administered questionnaire. The areas of interest included the manager's overall work environment, job satisfaction, one's relationship to the company's employment practices, one's views and attitudes about opportunities for Black managers, White views and attitudes toward Blacks, and other areas. The data showed that companies with a positive attitude toward affirmative action had effective and specific goal-setting plans in place.

Firms that registered a belief that the government was pressuring them to move faster than they wanted were firms that did not have plans with specific goals and did not show a true commitment to work force parity. The data provided evidence that discriminatory practices were more pronounced in these firms. Seventy percent plus of the Black managers surveyed did not believe Blacks had equity with

Whites in the corporate world. The primary factor by which company programs differed was their relative inconsistency in the application of affirmative action. Social pressure and economic consequences mandated by the government were the primary reasons given to explain why companies began to address the problem. The data indicated that there was clear evidence of differences in understanding of what affirmative action really meant.

It is clear from the above study that if you were Black, to obtain a promotion to a management position in Corporate America in the early 1970s was very difficult. During this period, WRS applied for numerous opportunities for managerial positions which were consistent with his background, skill level, and experience. WRS also believed, based upon his knowledge of his competition, that his chances were very good on a few occasions. He experienced difficulty in being seriously considered. It became difficult, after a number of lost opportunities, to understand the criteria by which the selections were made. The explanations given to explain the selection criteria were difficult to understand and did not appear to be logical. His careful study of how candidate selections were made revealed to him that there was more to the selection criteria than a person's qualifications. This conclusion began a valuable learning experience during WRS's attempts to obtain his first managerial assignment.

Several tactics employed in his attempts will be described next. WRS had spent a number of years in engineering. He had held titles of an associate engineer, engineer, and senior engineer. He had also transferred to marketing to acquire cross-functional experience. In marketing, he gained experience in developing business plans and learned strategic planning. He had demonstrated good performance in each of the functional areas. After a couple of years in the marketing department, he had expressed a desire to become a manager. After several unsuccessful opportunities competing against others who he felt were less qualified, he learned another tactic.

During a year-end company party, WRS met Dave Culley, his vice president/general manager. Dave Culley was young by comparison to other division general managers. He was thirty-two years old, very tall, clean-shaven, and had quickly advanced up the corporate ladder. He was well respected and was viewed by many as having the potential to become the CEO of the entire company. It seemed like an appropriate time to ask him questions concerning his management philosophy. Since no one on Dave's staff had a beard or moustache and WRS had both, WRS wondered if it made a difference whether Dave would have approved of a manager in his organization wearing a beard or moustache. WRS asked Dave what role physical appearance had in his selection of new managers. He indicated that it did not make a difference and immediately made a proposal to WRS. He proposed, to make his point, that he would grow a beard and a moustache. He also proposed that he would wear them for two months prior to year-end. He concluded his proposal by suggestioning that WRS take him to dinner upon keeping his word. If he didn't, he would take WRS to dinner. WRS was surprised by the proposal and accepted his general manager's offer. WRS felt the message was quite clear that physical appearance (beard or moustache) did not influence the selection of managers.

The year went by very quickly. WRS had observed by the end of the year that Dave had not lived up to his proposal and he became curious as to the reason. Due to their relative positions, he did not feel comfortable reminding the general manager of his wager. An additional eight months had passed before WRS saw the general manager. He was visiting employee groups while shaking hands and talking to them. When WRS and his general manager came in contact, they shared greetings and began to talk about the business. At the end of the conversation, WRS reminded Dave of his wager. Dave responded immediately saying that he remembered his proposal. WRS, being surprised that he remembered the proposal so vividly, dropped the subject. They continued to talk about other aspects of the business and then Dave soon departed.

In the ensuing weeks, WRS reflected upon the recent conversation he had with Dave. He also relived the twenty months and the original conversation he had had with Dave. He was determined to find out if there was a lesson to be learned from this experience. He concluded there was and for some reason Dave elected not to communicate it directly but chose a more subtle way. WRS removed his beard and his moustache.

Over the next few months, WRS continued to apply for managerial positions as they became available. Within six months, he was offered his first managerial assignment. WRS frequently remembers the incident he had with Dave. He has never been able to determine whether or not there was a connection between the shaving of his beard and the subsequent promotion. He and his general manager have never since corresponded on the subject. This connection has always remained a mystery.

The image of a corporate executive then could best be described as tall, well-dressed, White, male, and clean-shaven. In the corporate environment one rarely came into contact with executives having either a beard or a moustache. It was in the best interest of Blacks to imitate the corporate image as best as they could in order to enhance their chance of success. Appearance was used as an important factor in discrimination. Decision makers prejudge your ability to perform in a job based on your image. This is a point which many Black professionals miss as they compete for managerial assignments.

D. The First Managerial Assignment

The most frequently referenced article about what it was like to be a Black manager was written by Everett W. Jones, Jr. (1973). Jones was one of the first Black managers to document his experiences of what it was like to be Black in Corporate America. He observed that equal opportunity was more than just putting a Black man in a White man's job. He experienced a failure of his company to provide the needed organizational support after recruiting him. He generalized, based on his experience, that corporations will act as if the environment in which Blacks work is not color-sensitive and no further support is required to help them advance. He pointed out that due to his uniqueness he felt very isolated within the corporate setting. He stated: "The world of White business presented me with an elaborate socio-political organization that required unfamiliar codes of behavior" (p. 113). His experience left him with the uncertainty of being able to differentiate between problems that were attributable to him as a person, as a manager, or as a Black man.

WRS shared very similar experiences as Jones. WRS likened his first supervisory assignment to being a target in a shooting gallery. He found himself constantly moving back and forth while someone was constantly taking shots at him trying to derail or discredit him as a manager. In his first assignment, WRS was in charge of a subsection of fifteen all-White professionals. In addition, they were older, with many more years of experience in the corporate setting. WRS was resented. He was concerned that he would not last long.

WRS's first challenge was to understand the new dimensions of his responsibility. He did not have experience in dealing with this type of conflict. This situation posed a challenge and it was left up to him to demonstrate his skills. The problem between him and his staff was further exacerbated by the differences in their cultural framework. This represented a source of trust questions. A high degree of conflict persisted within the department. He was challenged in his ability to resolve conflict. His challenge was to instill respect, trust, and confidence in the subunit. This was accomplished with the help of one of his most vocal employee critics. The following is an approach which turned out to be very effective.

The subtle conflict between him and his staff continued for five months. Productivity had declined, and it also appeared inevitable that he would show poor performance in his first year in management. His most vocal critic was an employee in his late fifties who had been employed over thirty years. The employee would frequently belittle WRS's power by reminding WRS that WRS had less experience than he had. The employee was very antagonistic and frequently flirted with insubordination. The challenge was to turn this situation around. Since this particular employee was an informal leader, the strategy was to gain his support. WRS set up a meeting with him to obtain his advice as to how the unit could increase its overall performance. This was a covert action. WRS's objective was to recommend to him to become a lead person for the subunit. This action, WRS believed, would result in obtaining his support while also becoming an ally to assist WRS in obtaining the support from the rest of the unit.

WRS requested a meeting with the employee in WRS's office. Upon arriving the employee's greeting was less than cordial. This was consistent with his behavior because he always acted as if he were being inconvenienced. WRS requested his inputs as to how to improve the performance of the subunit. His subordinate began to list a number of actions that were needed. He also discussed the actions in such a way that made it difficult for WRS to understand them. He knew WRS had little knowledge of or experience in the specific actions identified. After an hour of discussion, the meeting had apparently produced an exhaustive list of well-structured, concise, and very doable strategies. They concluded that the list encompassed the most important things to do.

During the end of this process, WRS indicated that he would have difficulty trying to manage the unit through the strategies identified. WRS then asked his subordinate if he had any ideas as to how they could go about implementing the strategies. He very quickly responded that he did not because it would require a great deal of knowledge and experience. WRS agreed with him. WRS told him that they needed the best possible leader and suggested to his subordinate to take the assignment. WRS pointed out to him that he had the most knowledge as to how the strategies should be implemented. WRS further indicated that if he accepted, WRS would not approve of any action without obtaining his agreement. His subordinate was flabbergasted by this. He could not believe WRS would empower him to provide such leadership in the unit. He accepted the challenge immediately.

The above action by WRS resulted in instant respect, trust, and admiration from his subordinate. The subordinate returned to his desk as WRS's biggest fan. The subordinate quickly took the informal leadership role of the unit. Other employees began to observe his involvement, and responded in kind. He became recognized as an excellent informal leader and was proud of it. He began to speak very highly of WRS with others. This turn of events improved WRS's image and the performance of the unit also began to improve. During the following six months, the unit had improved sufficiently to where WRS's first performance review as manager was rated above average.

If a manager or subordinate wants to get one's way in a given situation, each must have or develop a *position of strength* over the other. This *position of strength* is the source of power to be used to exert influence over the other. A manager typically has *position power* over his subordinates. A subordinate is faced with either developing a *critical skill (knowledge power)* or becoming a powerful *informal leader* within the organization. In either case, it makes him essential to the success of the manager or company. If one has a greater power over the other, it will become a potential source of conflict. Trust existing between the two will keep the power advantage in balance.

This was an important lesson which was learned by WRS at a critical time. He learned that in order to build a strong team, one does not always have to project one's self as the team leader. If one empowers others to accomplish the task and provides reward and recognition for a job well done, the leader will ultimately benefit. His subordinate's energies had been channeled on the problem rather than against his manager. The subordinate later retired, feeling that WRS was the first manager who entrusted him to use his own judgment and expertise to carry out his tasks. This situation ended in a win/win solution for both.

E. Working for a Racist Manager

WRS was exposed to a situation of overt racism early in his career. He started his career as an engineer. During this period, he acquired a strong desire to become a manager which required experience in different functional areas. After reaching a project management level in engineering, he was offered a marketing position. Marketing was his first exposure to individuals on a management team who always seemed to have a hidden agenda.

After three years in marketing, WRS received a promotion to sub-section marketing manager. He was the first Black executive to have reached this level in the division. He was very pleased with this recognition. The hiring manager was a very personable individual, quite sensitive to affirmative action initiatives and fair play. The manager, after a short time, was promoted and a replacement was soon found. This began the difficulty for WRS.

The new manager was a racist. This was not obvious at first. The manager acted in ways which were very difficult to interpret. This made performing very challenging for WRS. He began to have difficulty in responding to the requirements of his job. WRS perceived that his manager did not want him to remain in his position. This, then, became a preoccupation of WRS during the first six months of this relationship. It became obvious that his manager treated him differently from his other staff. There was increased pressure on WRS to perform to higher standards which were dictated and not jointly agreed. WRS had received a very harsh assessment of his performance. The manager would frequently call WRS at home and request that he abruptly make plans to travel for great distances to work on issues which could have otherwise been satisfied locally. WRS refrained from discussing his problem with his manager. He wanted to avoid confrontation for fear it could have led to dismissal. WRS continued to act in ways which he felt were in the best interest of his career. This resulted in a complete adherence to whatever his manager requested.

After a year in the relationship, a situation arose which seemed ideal to discuss the problem with his manager. They were together at a sales meeting. It was late in the evening and they were alone and decided to have cocktails together at the bar. The atmosphere seemed relaxed and WRS had mustered the courage. WRS asked his manager why he was treating him so differently from the rest of his staff? The manager, for whatever reason, seemed compelled to answer the question. He stated: "I don't like Black people and you need to know that." This response was WRS's first exposure to overt racism. His manager went on to say that he was planning to reorganize the marketing section and the reorganization would affect WRS's reporting line. This change would result in WRS reporting to a new manager who would be layered between them. This situation started an intense effort by WRS to solve this dilemma. His objective was to determine how he could neutralize his section head's strong attitude against Blacks and somehow turn the relationship to a positive one.

Over the next six months, WRS did everything he could to ensure his performance was at or above his manager's expectations. He made certain he acted in ways that did not appear to be confronting the issue. He continued to demonstrate the unique capabilities he had and the advantages he brought to the organization. These actions were met with increased resistance by his manager. Over a period of time, it became clear that no matter what was done, his manager would not respond positively and would continue to apply pressure to ensure WRS's failure. The manager's continued insensitivity, racial attitude, and prejudicial acts caused WRS to alter his career plans. WRS left the company at the conclusion of eight years of service. It was clear his manager was a barrier for him, and without a conflict resolution alternative within the company, he felt the better choice was to seek a better work environment.

This experience helped to build WRS's character. A blatant exposure to racism within corporations is a reality of the Black corporate life. Racism was a reality within our society, why shouldn't it be the same within Corporate America? Interacting with people on a professional level certainly did not make a difference—why should it? Corporations are a subset of the larger environment. Confronting racism in our society was bringing about change. Confronting racism in corporations, however, was not in the best interest of WRS. During this time there were only a few Black professionals in management. Conflict resolution alternatives for racial issues were not in place. The alternative of uniting with other Blacks and creating a larger group with common issues was also not an alternative, since there were few Black professional associations.

WRS's subordinates, as mentioned above, were all White professionals, older and with more experience in the business. This exacerbated the problem. Their acceptance of him was tentative, creating an environment that was questionable at best. One can only speculate that a Black professional within a White majority work environment without any support (White or Black) would have a high potential for failure. WRS's main concern was that one complaint could have been interpreted by the White majority that Black professionals could not cope in the corporate environment. They were right, but for the wrong reasons.

Wells and Jennings's (1984) research on White reactions to Black career advancement advanced the notion that White reactions are remnants of "Herrenvolk"[1] democracy. They were concerned with four things: the career disparity that exists between Blacks and their White peers, how organizational barriers deter Blacks as a group from fulfilling their ambitions, how White reactions and resistance to the advent of Black career advancements occur, and the lack of adequate theoretical models that explain the creation and maintenance of systemic barriers that exclude Blacks. Their concept of labor-force proportion adds to the collage of racism within the corporate setting.

As Blacks attempt to advance their careers, the emergence of tension occurs and blocking and tackling are done to keep Blacks lower in the organization. Wells and Jennings state: "The middle managers must maintain the illusion of [equal treatment]. Ultimately this results in the deterrence of Blacks through attrition or the creation of organizational conditions and managerial practices that some Blacks find intolerable" (p. 46). This attrition creates a gap and White managers use this gap to explain why Blacks are not in higher levels of the organization. They state: "Given the dynamics of this illustration, the outcomes are quite predictable. The White management structure can point to the high attrition of Blacks as evidence of Black inferiority and unworthiness of special affirmative action programs" (p. 46). (See Figure 5 on p. 82)

Racism in corporations is commonly experienced by most Black professional employees, and even more so by Black professionals who are upward-mobile and who are motivated to achieve higher-level management positions. In order to reach a high-level position in Corporate America, one inevitably will be exposed to the "racist manager." This is a manager who practices racism openly and will tell a Black how he feels about him and his kind. Direct exposure by a Black professional to this type of manager can be very unnerving. He is in a double bind. On the one hand, if he were to confront such a manager and/or seek alternatives to resolve the conflict, he could possibly be viewed by the White majority as overreacting to his environment. Another view is he is too sensitive to what is typically viewed as a very normal situation. On the other hand, if left unchallenged, the Black professional will typically become withdrawn, very preoccupied with the negative environment, and his productivity will be impaired. This represents a dilemma for Black employees.

NOTE

1. Herrenvolk is the German term that usually refers to the Aryan "master race" and White men in particular. Hence a Herrenvolk democracy is a regime designed to protect the rights and privileges of a master race of White men.

Chapter 5

Corporate America, Part II (1978–1990): A Repertoire of Insights

A. Introduction: The Environment

Corporate America Part II presents a new start for WRS. He joined a new company in order to continue along his career path. He left the racist manager who was in his career path hoping that it was a once-in-a-lifetime experience. His corporate life during 1978–1990 provided new challenges.

During this period major macro trends were demanding a greater ability on the part of managers and leaders to resolve increasing conflict in the work environment. The conflict arose from a number of different sources such as competitive pressures, improved responsiveness, and the need for better performing and higher quality products. New technology introduced into the company's way of doing business had an influence on the process and caught many employees off-guard. Some employees were not well trained or prepared to respond to the changing technological challenges. Uncertainty about their future and inability to grasp new ways of doing things were the predominant concerns.

Changing demographics also brought more diversification into the work environment and caused increased cultural unrest. This latter challenge was the newest and perhaps the most difficult to resolve. Cultural diversity in society had caused racial unrest for many years, necessitating legislation to bring about social order. Dealing with similar unrest within the work environment was requiring managerial development that was not being emphasized in university-level training. Many corporations during this period were taking it upon themselves to teach managers and employees how to manage cultural diversity. Although many companies had been slow to recognize that this important change was impacting their financial results, some began to believe a focus in this area would create an opportunity to reap immediate financial returns.

In order to assimilate into the corporate work environment, Blacks had to overcome an image problem as well as racism. Blacks were slow to understand how their dress and other physical attributes made them stand out. WRS was fortunate to recognize the subtle message of his general manager. The elimination of his beard and moustache was only the beginning. There were also questions as to whether Black professionals possessed the skills to handle tough business interactions such as negotiations. Blacks were also viewed as aggressive and were not patient about the slow advancement one encounters in Corporate America. Blacks were purposefully brought along more slowly because it was felt that they lacked the needed training and exposure to deal with corporate life—exposure to such things as the ambiguity associated with the complexity of properly reading their environment. Furthermore, a tremendous fear existed among Whites that if Blacks were given high-level executive positions, they would fail. It was believed that Blacks did not have the political skills required. Whites who were in a position to select Blacks for high-level positions were also concerned about how it would affect them if

Blacks whom they selected would fail. There were more lessons to be learned.

B. Dressing for Success

There are a number of different criteria used to evaluate one's acceptability within the corporate structure. Some may rank very low on the executive's scale. An executive should use the clothing style favored by his superiors and peers as a guide to how he should dress. Wearing the latest fashions may not always be in the best interests of one's career growth. There is, in fact, an unwritten code, and the concern here is dress code in the corporate environment.

WRS, as a new manager, encountered a situation involving image with Mr. B. Mr. B. had recruited WRS and had assigned him an executive job in Marketing. In a performance review given to WRS, there was a dimension to it which was unexpected. His manager critiqued his choice of clothing. The environment was very conservative and many managers dressed in dark conservative attire. WRS's attire, although well-balanced in choice of colors and styling, made him stand out from the other executives. This created some concern. Mr. B. had the challenge of dealing with this sensitive issue. He told WRS, during a performance review, that he should consider buying a new wardrobe—one that was more consistent with that of the other executives. This was a new learning experience for WRS.

Blacks do not harbor the same values and styles as their White counterparts in the work environment. Blacks' preference in attire is influenced by their desire to express themselves. Blacks view their clothes as an extension of themselves. Typically, the choice is made to establish uniqueness rather than uniformity.

This feedback to WRS had an impact on his feeling of "fit" within the environment. After eight years in Corporate America, it was the first time this issue had surfaced. The issue heightened WRS's level of awareness and sensitivity to a new dimension. WRS became more keenly aware of the clothes other executives were wearing in the work environment. He studied the relationship of the style of dress of executives who were at higher levels within the organization to those who were at lower positions. It was also important to compare executives who were viewed as leaders with high growth potential to those who were not. These observations, much to his amazement, clearly correlated. A valid relationship was discerned among the variables of level in the organizations, a good image, and being considered a "well dressed" executive. Outward appearance, he concluded, was a significant factor in career advancement, image, and acceptability within the corporate ranks.

C. The Art of Negotiating

In order to enhance one's chances of succeeding in the business environment, one must develop good negotiating skills. This, very simply, means the ability to interact with others in such a way that when differences exist, one can create a win/win environment. WRS's skills were tested during a major negotiation which had high corporate visibility and involved the negotiation of a valuable company contract. This was a critical test case. Positioning WRS to be the negotiator was set up by WRS's manager (Mr. B.). Can WRS really succeed in a tough negotiation of high importance? Can he deal with the stress? Can he maneuver? Can he exercise good communication skills? Does he understand how to arrive at a successful financial outcome? Does he understand business? Can he produce results? These were just a few of the questions which, he believed, were on his manager's mind. The questions were waiting to be answered by the outcome of this negotiation. This was a very exciting as well as a nervous time for WRS. He knew that he was under the spotlight and the results of the negotiation with Bosch (a German automotive company), could significantly influence his career. He was sent to Germany by his manager to be responsible for and achieve a successful outcome to a very sensitive and important situation.

The negotiations with Bosch included a very large contract for automobile electronic ignition systems. Bosch's executives arrived at the negotiation table well prepared. Since Bosch was the customer, they seemed to be holding all the cards. WRS and a local salesperson were the only ones representing their company, while the Bosch negotiating team consisted of six senior level executive managers. They were well known for high skill at reducing price and "demolishing" a vendor.

The negotiation was planned to last for a day but continued for two days. At the end of the first day, WRS was emotionally and mentally drained, with the outcome still in question. The second day of the negotiation was also WRS's birthday. Bosch's negotiating team knew this and presented him with a cake and a gift at the beginning of the negotiation. What an interesting ploy. Their tactic was to lengthen what was already going to be a long and a very difficult day. The negotiations were extremely difficult. There were many compromises, but in the end the outcome was a win/win.

This story is important to the case study because it established a high degree of credibility for WRS in his new company. It was another major hurdle WRS had to cross. He had to demonstrate to his manager and peers that if given the opportunity, he could successfully deal with a very complicated and a very sensitive business issue. Upon returning to the division, WRS's accomplishments were applauded. The letter shown in Figure 3 was widely circulated.

15 November 1979

Personal

Mr. B
MICRO SWITCH
A Division of
HONEYWELL Inc.
11 West Spring Street
Freeport/Illinois 61032
U.S.A.

BOSCH - '79 and '80 Contract Negotiations

Dear Mr. B,

Referencing our contract negotiations with BOSCH on 7 and 8 November '79 I wish to compliment you on the outstanding performance of Bill Spivey. A very major portion of us reaching an agreement with BOSCH can be attributed to Bill's excellent skills negotiating a major contract with an automotive customer. It was very apparent that his many years experience in negotiating was key to our success. The objectives given were so far away from what BOSCH anticipated that a great deal of sensitiveness and sense of responsibility was required to sell our position without upsetting the customer and destroying a good business relationship which was built over a period of five years.

I was very impressed with Bill's knowledge, enthusiasm and dedication and like to pass on my sincere thanks for providing such key individual to negotiate the contracts with BOSCH.

Let me also pass on thanks to all other people in marketing, engineering, production control and customer service who all have made inputs and many personal efforts to get this business.

Figure 3

The successful outcome to the negotiations, a truly important milestone in WRS's career, brought immediate credibility to WRS.

D. Bringing One Along Slowly

Fernandez (1975) identified in a study the reason almost exclusively used by White managers as to why there were not more Blacks in business. They are:

- *The cultural argument:* Blacks lack the necessary entrepreneurial attitude or the ambition, initiative, and dependability for success in the business world. Furthermore, the argument goes, that Blacks' life-style makes them unable to fit well into corporate life.
- *The qualification argument:* Blacks lack the educational achievement and other necessary qualifications, such as experience in technical know-how, to rise in business.
- And finally, the third category, which the author acknowledges, is broader than the above two while encompassing them both: *racial discrimination* (p. 79).

The first two are explanatory arguments that tend to justify Whites' behavior toward Blacks and why they feel the way they do. The common belief shared by both the Black and White managers in the study was that Black managers need higher qualifications than their White counterparts in order to succeed in similar jobs. The responses also indicated that Whites were afraid to promote Blacks due to their belief that they will fail. This attitude fosters their belief that the cultural upbringing of Blacks is not suitable for business.

The authors conclude:

It is quite obvious from the material presented in this [report] that real equal employment opportunities for Blacks still do not exist. One of the most pervasive of American myths holds that, in this land, regardless of race, creed, color, or national origin, one can get ahead solely on his or her abilities (p. 93).

Being patient is one of the most important abilities for Blacks to develop in Corporate America. Large companies seem to move slowly in responding to environmental changes. Since career advancement does take time, however, it can sometimes be a tactic used by majority managers to discriminate. Many Black professionals are sensitive to this tactic, which often became a source of conflict. There are variations by industry as to the amount and type of experience required for executive level positions. In the electronic industry, for example, one may encounter younger executives at higher levels than in the machine tool or the automotive industries. In the electronic industry, where WRS began his corporate career, reaching the level of general manager when one was in his early thirties was commonplace. In the industrial sector, where WRS transferred to, the average age for similar positions was the late thirties. WRS also observed that the average age for a Black executive for equivalent positions was even higher. This reality also applied to him.

At the beginning of WRS's career, he established an objective of becoming a general manager of an electronics oriented business by the time he was thirty-five. Based on the age of the general managers he knew, it appeared to be a very reasonable objective for the electronics industry. His general manager at the time was thirty-two years old and had been in his position for two years. After establishing the objective, WRS carefully identified his strategy for achieving it. His plan included working in two or more disciplines (Engineering, Manufacturing, or Marketing). While acquiring experience in multiple disciplines was the right choice, there were unanticipated changes that impacted the timing. One change, discussed above, was necessitated by the incident with the racist manager. This resulted in WRS moving from the electronic to the industrial industry. However, this was not the entire story. WRS was thirty-one when he changed companies. His first position was as a marketing manager with considerably less responsibility than in his previous job. At thirty-two he had reached a director-level position. The successful Bosch negotiation had paid off. By this single accomplishment, he was able to get back on the time target toward achieving his objective. The first director-level position was Marketing. After eighteen months, he was promoted to Director of Engineering. The Marketing and Engineering assignments were both consistent with his objective to build his experience in different areas. They were very challenging assignments and he performed very well in them. He became recognized as a good leader and a candidate for higher-level positions. He was thirty-six when the first general management opportunity occurred. This was perfect timing.

The business in which WRS worked had performed very well and his general manager was promoted to a more senior position. It was a unique opportunity for WRS. He had developed a very strong relationship with his manager during the previous three years. WRS's performance reviews with his manager confirmed that he was viewed as being highly talented and was in line for a general management position. He was in an ideal position. He had worked in the business unit for three years. He had served in two of the four positions which reported to the general manager.

He had performed well in both positions. He understood the breadth and depth of the general manager's position. In addition, he had compared himself to his known competitors and concluded that he was in the best position. His interview for the general management opportunity was revealing.

During the session, it became obvious by the interviewer's lack of enthusiasm and excitement that WRS's chances of being selected were remote. The following was a statement which supported his feelings: "WRS, as you know, in order to develop a championship boxer, you need to bring him along slowly. You need to make certain he is ready for the championship fight. This approach is what I have planned for you." Having listened to this, WRS wondered about the implications of this philosophy to his career. The job opening was ideal. WRS had a reputation as a leader within the business unit and had the respect of his peers and subordinates. The employees in the business unit had anticipated that WRS would be selected. If only they knew what the grand plan was. WRS was not selected for the position.

The following two years were difficult. The business unit experienced a number of business issues. The markets the business unit served were soft and major technical problems were experienced. The vice president of his business unit was later reassigned to another position. This action made the vice presidential position available again. Ironically WRS interviewed for a second time with the same person as two years earlier.

During the previous two years, he had worked as the Director of Engineering. He had been given two performance reviews, both of which were excellent. He had clearly demonstrated cross-functional leadership and had positively added to his experience. The past two years had confirmed, in his view, that he was ready for the vice presidential position. Again he was excited about the opportunity and felt that he was the best candidate for the job. During the interviewing process, there did not appear to be any obstacles or possible derailment factors. He was asked to give an update about how he felt about his performance for the previous two years. He also explained why he felt he was the right person for the job. Again the job opening was to manage the business unit in which he was already involved. He appeared to be an obvious choice. If WRS were chosen, it would have provided continuity to the organization. The interview was quite comprehensive and he had a high degree of confidence of being selected.

Over the following few weeks, the selection process was concluded. The senior vice president had selected an alternate candidate whom no one within the division or business unit knew. The selection was a shock to others within the business unit. There was no obvious explanation as to why the division's senior vice president selected someone with no prior experience managing a highly technical organization. Similar to the previous selection, this individual did not have knowledge of the overall business. The feedback WRS received from the senior vice president was that while WRS was an excellent candidate, his selection was someone else. WRS was told to continue along the aggressive track he had been on, keep his motivational level high, and he would be considered again for future opportunities.

Again, WRS could not develop a logical rationale as to why he was not selected. Two very important observations WRS made which were common to both selections were that the persons selected had an excellent network of friends and allies within the corporation. In addition, they each had a high-level mentor. These observations gave WRS clues about his next strategy.

Within a short time, WRS was reassigned as Director of

Operations within the same business unit. The assignment completed the list of possible assignments below the vice-presidential level. There were no other assignments at the director level which would have been viable as a next career move. At the end of two and a half years, the opportunity for the same vice president and general manager position became available. The vice president of the unit was promoted, allowing WRS, once again, an opportunity to become a vice president.

The interviewing process this time was different. WRS had learned a lesson from prior unsuccessful attempts. He had continued to demonstrate excellent performance as a leader in the different functional areas. In addition, he had developed a network of stakeholders who were aware of his talent and his desire to be promoted. He had established an excellent track record in dealing effectively with difficult technical, factory, and marketing problems. He had demonstrated a persistent attitude and patience. It was well known that this was his third attempt for this position. The last key difference was the interviewer. The business had been restructured under a different senior executive, who had a reputation for taking a much more liberal viewpoint when promoting people. The interview was brief and extremely positive. WRS's networking was the key. He decided to select WRS without any reservations. The offer was extended at the end of the interview.

To remain patient when one has a feeling that one is experiencing racial bias is difficult. This was a concern WRS had with the previous two choices. In each case, there was no clear evidence as to why the selections were made. The selections raised questions of trust and unfair managerial practices. It also was not clear that the interviewer in the first two cases had the final say-so in the selection process.

In corporations, the one who has the power or the control was not always obvious. When WRS was selected, it seemed clear who the decision maker was. The interviewer exhibited full control and power to make the selection. In either case, the added knowledge WRS gained with this experience was valuable. Networking played a very influential part in WRS's strategy. He developed allies at many levels within the organization. He obtained, through his networking, a mentor. The mentor helped in the navigational process.

A key lesson learned is how corporate decision making is done. The criteria used in selecting individuals for top-level jobs are not always obvious. One should not take for granted that prior experience, demonstrated performance, and education are the only ingredients needed to succeed. Although "what" you know is important, "who" you know seems to play a much more significant role. This was a major point for WRS to learn as he developed his strategy to advance his career in Corporate America.

E. Being Managed by Intimidation

Nixon's (1980) study determined whether Black managers surveyed felt alienated or integrated within Corporate America. She developed what was called a "corporate fit scale" to determine what percentages of the managers felt they were included (and to what degree) in full participation and acceptance in the corporate setting. In a separate study, Nixon (1980) evaluated Black managers' perceptions of job power within the corporate setting. Both studies provided mixed results and were inconclusive as to how these results would differ from White managers' when asked similar questions. The data from the first study revealed that 12% of the managers perceived a low degree of corporate fit. They were classified as alienated based on their extreme position on the integration/alienation continuum. Nixon defined the alienated experience as exclusion from full participation and acceptance in a corporate setting. The data also revealed that 44% of the managers perceived a moderate degree of corporate fit. They were classified as between full participation and acceptance and total exclusion in corporate life. The balance, 44%, perceived a high degree of corporate fit. These managers were viewed as feeling totally integrated and totally accepted within their White-dominated corporations.

It is rare for one to advance in corporations without encountering some extreme managerial style. In this case, one manager managed by intimidation, creating fear in employees. Using this style of management with Black professionals adds to the problems they already have in the work environment. WRS experienced a high degree of alienation under this particular manager. During this period, there was significant tension and anxiety in the relationship. This manager is referred to as Mr. X.

Mr. X was viewed by the corporation as a highly talented corporate executive. Interacting with Mr. X's style would have challenged the brightest and the most talented of subordinates. In order to survive this management style, knowing when to be humble was important. WRS had to behave in ways which constantly played to Mr. X's ego. He was not able to exercise his own style for fear of a confrontation. This proved successful.

If Blacks react confrontationally to this style of intimidation, it would usually result in their becoming the victim. Typically, when a Black reacts in a confrontational style, he is viewed as being defensive, insensitive to the environment, not a team player, or as one who simply cannot adjust to the corporate environment. It requires a high level of skill to first recognize when one must adjust one's behavior to maintain a positive relationship.

Executives who manage Black employees are not always sensitive to the many dimensions of their (the executives') problem. White executives were not sensitive to their own prejudices and the bias which they have when decisions involving Blacks were made. Mr. X's management style frequently caused alienation and possibly turnover because it was felt by many Blacks to be the "straw that broke the camel's back."

Although it was a trying time, WRS received excellent experience as a result of being managed by Mr. X. It improved his "navigational" skills and hardened his "armor." The experience tested his ability to tolerate bias, stress, intimidation, and the exploitative use of managerial power. Experiencing this management style without breaking elevated WRS to a new level of political skill. He had experienced the worst management style to date. WRS knew that he must learn to cope with managers like this. They are commonplace in the environment. WRS learned that the realities of corporate life should never be underestimated.

F. Building Trust

The significance of the establishment of trust through positioning supports the notion that leaders should exhibit consistency in their behavior. A consistent pattern over long periods of time establishes a sense of reliability and prediction. To be sure, there will always be opportunities that challenge a leader's behavior. Adverse situations may arise that may bring about a tendency for the leader to change behavior in ways that are not consistent with the established pattern. This inconsistency in behavior could raise trust questions from within the organization.

The leader should be aware that employees generally will operate on the basis of perception versus reality. To them, what they perceive is their reality. As a rule of thumb, a leader should spend more time getting in tune with a subordinate's perception rather than relying on his own.

As WRS reflected on the numerous incidents that had occurred over his first two years as the general manager, none stood out as much as the one that caused the division's progress to stall and begin to regress. The following identifies what is believed to have been the watershed event that helped turn the division from a nonprofitable business operation to a success.

In order to build a successful organization, the leader should establish a solid foundation of trust. By the time WRS was promoted to division Vice President/General Manager, he had spent nearly ten years in various executive positions within the organization, and had accumulated experience as well as the demonstrated ability to successfully lead many of the functional areas. He was very comfortable developing his executives to be effective leaders in their positions. As the General Manager, he spent a great deal of time working with his subordinates on details in their various areas. He tried to demonstrate by example how to resolve problems. The perception he had of his actions was that of helping and teaching. He constantly exhibited a willingness to get involved in very detailed aspects of his subordinates' jobs. This, he believed, was a very welcome form of help.

Over time, WRS sensed social distance emerging between his staff and him. At the staff level, productivity began to wane as a result of a lack of cohesive teamwork. Troubled by this, he decided to ask his staff to give him a performance review during one of his staff meetings. After he created a conducive environment, his staff began to list their concerns. The one concern that emerged time and time again was their resentment of his involvement in the details of their various functions. When he asked them to tell him why they resented his involvement, since he was only trying to help, their unanimous response was that his involvement was perceived by them as a lack of trust by him in their abilities. WRS was shocked at the perception they had. After the meeting, he began to act in ways that exhibited trust through positioning. He kept out of the detailed day-to-day operations of the various functions, and empowered and entrusted his executives to accomplish the various tasks. Eventually a very strong and dedicated team emerged.

In the above example, in the early going, a foundation of trust had not been established between WRS and his staff. As a result, WRS's staff and the rest of the organization were not effective. Trust was a very valuable missing resource which was a critical ingredient needed for WRS's success and the success of the division. It was WRS's premise that establishing and replenishing a foundation of trust was a prerequisite to organizational success. It should be the starting point for the building of a strong organization. Trust, as a resource, was instituted to foster teamwork, higher creativity, higher productivity, a positive work environment, higher commitment, and loyalty. To be sure, an organization with the aforementioned ingredients will have the benefits of reduced costs, improved quality, and overall better company performance than it would otherwise.

WRS learned that the leader of the organization should recognize that effective communication and consistent behavior went a long way toward helping his subordinates have trust. Trust must be earned and it should not be taken for granted. Once he acquired it, he cherished it and replenished it as an important foundation to his and the organization's integrity.

G. You're the General Manager, Sink or Swim: The Art of Empowering

To permit acknowledgment, leaders should disclose the bases of their managerial actions. This will give the organization a frame of reference by which to judge their actions. Trust rests on acknowledged competence. Leaders should empower their work force members. Empowerment provides a sense of being for any individual that allows them to believe that they can achieve their dreams and ambitions. A sense of self-direction and self-achievement will allow an individual to contribute to an organization, but more importantly it builds their self-esteem, creates positive climates in the company, and allows them to make decisions and move forward with their roles and responsibilities. In the experience of WRS, being empowered by his manager was necessary for him to achieve the leadership and results in which he was held accountable.

Operating in the position of General Manager in Corporate America is very similar to being in business for yourself. If you don't do it, no one else will do it for you. You must be a self-starter and take the initiative to do whatever is professionally required to meet your commitments. If you do not perform on a consistent basis, failure is certain. If you do, you will be recognized and rewarded. This was clearly evident in WRS's first assignment as a general manager.

As mentioned above, being a general manager of a division within a large conglomerate is analogous to running your own business. You are viewed as an independent businessperson who establishes the business plan and delivers the results to the corporate headquarters. Success or failure depends upon how well you are able to establish yourself as the leader and deliver the agreed-upon objectives year after year. How one achieves the end results is also a key measurement. WRS was fortunate that his manager operated with an empowerment philosophy. WRS's manager extended trust at the beginning of their relationship and early in his new assignment. By extending trust, he gave a high vote of confidence in WRS's ability to perform at or above his expectations. WRS was highly motivated by this trusting style. WRS felt committed not to let his manager down, no matter what.

WRS's job situation was quite challenging. The headquarters and factories had to be relocated 1,500 miles. Many employees did not desire to relocate. The impact of losing many experienced employees caused a great deal of turmoil. The turmoil affected the morale and financial results of the operation. The greatest challenges were to build a cohesive team, add over 40% more employees to the work force, build trust in the work environment, train and develop people's skills, and resolve continuous ongoing conflict. There were a number of successes and failures during his first general management assignment. Since this was a division that was nonprofitable, WRS was assigned to turn it around.

The empowerment approach of WRS's manager allowed WRS to do what was required to accomplish the task. His manager's "sink or swim" approach proved to be very effective. It was a high-risk approach for his manager. If WRS had failed, it would have supported the many myths which existed about Blacks' ability to succeed in the corporate environment.

The division later received both the People and Growth Awards for 1989 shown in Figure 4.

PEOPLE

PRESENTED TO

KEYBOARD DIVISION

BILL SPIVEY

HONEYWELL MANAGEMENT MEETING

PHOENIX, ARIZONA

FEBRUARY 21-23, 1990

Dr. James J. Renier

CHAIRMAN &

CHIEF EXECUTIVE OFFICER

Honeywell

HELPING CONTROL YOUR WORLD

GROWTH

PRESENTED TO

KEYBOARD DIVISION

BILL SPIVEY

HONEYWELL MANAGEMENT MEETING

PHOENIX, ARIZONA

FEBRUARY 21-23, 1990

Dr. James J. Renier

CHAIRMAN &

CHIEF EXECUTIVE OFFICER

Honeywell

HELPING CONTROL YOUR WORLD

Figure 4

Chapter 6

Summary Remarks on Succeeding in Corporate America

Advancing one's career in Corporate America in the 1980s and certainly in the 1990s was and will probably continue to be different from what it was in the 1960s and 1970s, especially if one is Black or a female. Although Black awareness and female importance in the work force has increased through EEO and DWF initiatives[1], other obstacles have crept in that are less apparent. The discussion here will start with the meaning of the term "Corporate America," which can be described in many ways. WRS's perception of his corporate environment can best be summarized figuratively by the author as follows:

> It was like a jungle where the animals prey on each other for survival, where friend or foe do not present themselves in their obvious form, where swinging from one tree to the next becomes increasingly difficult as the vines you use become shorter and shorter and the distances between the trees increase.
> It was like a mirror maze, where dead ends seem to be around each corner and there doesn't appear to be a clear path to get to your goals and as you look in the mirrors along the way, your body takes on different shapes and

sizes as you ask yourself: "Is it still I that has traveled the lonely roads?"

It was like a Rubik's Cube where getting all the obstacles and opportunities properly grouped was a near impossibility.

It was like a crossword puzzle where planning is very key and trying to get education, experience and the right opportunities to intersect requires ingenuity sometimes beyond human belief.

It was like playing football against an extremely formidable team—and your own team is made up of people you thought you knew and could trust, but now that is not sure.

It was like walking through a minefield where one missed step can cost you your career.

It was like Russian Roulette where each blank represents an opportunity realized and each bullet could end your career.

It was like playing basketball where the hoop diameter is smaller than the ball and the hoop represents opportunities and you are the ball.

Taking a journey through Corporate America without a map can be quite fatal unless one knows all the paths to follow. Planning job changes for career growth follows an approach similar to that used in college. In order to obtain a degree, one's courses had to be planned in order to satisfy the requirements. One's career is the same way. They say that when a person purchases commercial real estate, the three things one must keep in mind are *location, location, location*. When one embarks on one's career, the three things one must keep in mind are *plan, plan, plan*. Plan one's education, plan one's positions, plan one's stakeholders.

How did WRS go about planning his career in light of the complexities that existed in Corporate America? Having specialized in low energy nuclear physics he was hired by General Electric for a special program which had been contracted with the federal government that required a special design/concept of a *lithium drift germanium detector*. He was classified as an engineer. He was nervous, confused about this new environment; nevertheless, it was the sacrifice he had to make in moving away from his comfort zone to a new environment. He was involved with the project for six months before he found himself out of a job. The program was cancelled by the government and, since he was a specialist, there weren't other jobs available that required his expertise. This was his welcome to Corporate America. He decided if this is the way of life in Corporate America, he would need to "protect himself at all times."

He seriously began a career planning exercise. He defined as his objective "to become a general manager of an electronic oriented business by age thirty-five." Having set his objective, the next step was to map out an action plan. In summary, the plan, aimed at becoming a general manager, was to develop a wider range of education and to work in disciplines other than engineering. He planned future assignments in engineering, engineering management, marketing, marketing management, manufacturing, and manufacturing management. During the next eighteen years, he accumulated six years in each area, including individual contributor and management assignments in each. He became a general manager of an electronic oriented business at forty. The point to this discussion is that WRS found career planning essential. Career planning to WRS was: 1) determining where he wanted to be in his career at some future period of time; 2) assessing what he had already accomplished; 3) reviewing his job experience and determining additional assignments he had to have; 4) determining who should be added to his stakeholder list and how the relationships should be cultivated; and 5) developing his time line. He established where he wanted to go, and how he planned to get there. Without the plan, his chances of reaching his goal would have been more remote. One must establish a goal and obtain the education and the experience required for it.

This required WRS to focus in a number of different areas:

(1) Education
(2) Experience
(3) Patience
(4) Networking
(5) Mentors
(6) Socializing
(7) Dress/Appearance
(8) Worldly knowledge
(9) Flexibility
(10) Traits/Skills, i.e., listening, speaking, political, reading body language, analytical
(11) Remaining successful

These eleven points may be compared to the Fernandez findings (see p. 53 above) of three factors:

- *The cultural argument:* Blacks lack the necessary entrepreneurial attitude or the ambition, initiative, and dependability for success in the business world. Furthermore, the argument goes, Blacks' life-style make them unable to fit well into corporate life.
- *The qualification argument:* Blacks lack the educational achievement and other necessary qualifications, such as experience in technical know-how, to rise in business.

- And finally, the third category, which, the author acknowledges, is broader than the above two, while encompassing them both: *racial discrimination* (p. 79).

Education: A college education is almost a requirement. Most companies were requiring advanced degrees either in a specific subject or in business education such as the content of an MBA degree. If one's goal is to become a specialist in a specific functional area such as Marketing, Engineering, Manufacturing, then education related to those specific functions would be the direction one would take. If one were interested in management, then an MBA degree would be helpful. WRS acquired his Master's degree in a technical field.

Experience: If one wanted to continue to specialize in a specific function and develop skills in a vertical fashion, it is important that one continue to expand one's experiences in a specialized discipline such as marketing, engineering, or the like. A logical path, in the case of engineering, would be an engineer, a senior engineer, a principal engineer, an engineering supervisor, an engineering manager, a director of engineering, a vice president of engineering, and so forth. To enhance one's potential for growth vertically in a discipline, a cross-company, cross-divisional, or international assignment would enhance one's ability to achieve the highest level. If, however, one pursues a management path such as general manager, then one should develop cross-functional training such as the path WRS followed, to begin to broaden one's experience.

One would, therefore, develop nonmanagerial experiences in various disciplines advancing to managerial assignments in one or more of the areas. The path WRS followed was cross-functional—changing from engineering to manufacturing, to marketing, to marketing management, to engineering management, to manufacturing management, to an operational assignment where he was managing more than one discipline, and then he was considered for general management.

Patience: There are times when one may be required to remain in a "holding pattern" until the right opportunity comes along. This happened to WRS. During his first year of transitioning to his second company, he was in a "holding pattern." He had joined the company as Marketing Manager for the Solid State Components group, and eight months later his company reorganized and eliminated his job. Later he was reassigned to a staff position. He was patient, and a year later he acquired a director-level position.

Networking is important. You must build a positive network of stakeholders. One does not succeed alone in Corporate America. The adage, "it is not what you know, but whom you know" is what WRS found out to be true. WRS can conclude, based on his experience, it is a combination of the "who" and the "what." Networking included developing friends and allies among people who recruit, clear a path, provide a reference, or could provide him with guidance as to how to attain his career goals. These people were in his work and his social environment. (See Appendix D for more discussion.)

WRS found that having a *mentor* is very important. His mentor was a high-level executive who took a personal interest in his well-being and played an influential role to facilitate job considerations and provided guidance. His mentor emerged from networking (people with whom he had established a positive relationship). Some corporations will assign an executive to high-potential individuals for the purpose of facilitating upward mobility. This did not happen in this case study, and one should not depend on being selected as a mentee.

WRS found *socializing* was a necessity within the corporate environment. Although not discussed in the case, he frequently was in a situation where he was participating in dinner meetings or other social situations. How he conducted himself during the social engagements was very important. WRS almost hurt his very positive career by a social interaction that was unfavorable. He learned that even in the social environment, he had to maintain his professionalism, remain career-minded, remain aware of his surroundings, and understand how perceptions evolve.

How one *dresses* and one's *appearance* reveals a lot. Some executives overlook attire as being unimportant. WRS recognized that he obviously could not change his race; however, his hairstyle and clothes were within his control. WRS had been one who wore the most recent fad in order to stand out and be recognized. The advice he received from his manager was invaluable. He changed—now dressing in harmony with his surroundings, no longer trying to be different from his peers or immediate superiors.

WRS learned that being *worldly* was an asset. This paid off while networking. There were broader expectations, he found out, for executives to have knowledge and views going beyond their professional expertise. This embodies an ability to converse in global terms concerning world economics, history, the future, politics, and so forth. He learned, however, to have neutral, noncontroversial views in many of these areas. Typically, he found that people are just not necessarily interested in one's specific position on various issues, but are more intent on determining that you have an awareness and an ability to discuss in generalities.

One must keep an open mind and be *flexible* to respond to new opportunities. Some opportunities did require WRS to relocate to an undesired geographical area or take on a special assignment. When receiving a staff assignment, he compromised and simply waited for the next opportunity. WRS remained flexible and kept an open mind to career options.

WRS learned that certain skills were very important to have in order to cope with in the corporate setting. Each, once learned and applied, helped him grow:

Good *listening skills* were extremely important. Early in his career, when he presented his research to his colleagues, he was not keenly listening to what they were saying. Becoming emotional has a way of blocking out very valuable information. His manager who was in the audience brought this to his attention. This was a lesson well learned. Many Black professionals who are not good listeners tend to answer questions not asked or misunderstand their basic intent. Good listening skills, moreover, will reveal that what one hears is not always the same as what is being communicated. When WRS was a Product Planner for his first company he reported to a Product Manager along with another Product Planner. The Manager gave each of the planners the same assignment. They both were in line for the Product Manager's position. WRS was very competitive— in this case, almost to a fault. He did exactly what the manager asked. In fact, he completed the task earlier than his manager had expected. During the process, he was also following what his competitor (the other planner), was doing. Based on his observations, he concluded that his competitor could not have listened to the instructions. After WRS had turned in his work, the Product Manager requested his presence in his office and his manager began to praise his competitor's work! He was shocked! When WRS asked about his, he was told to do it over. He asked what was the problem. The manager said WRS had given him what he had asked for; however, the other planner had given him what he had wanted. WRS learned a lesson. Many times people say what they mean but do not mean what they say—some mean what they say but do not say what they mean.

Political skills were the most difficult for WRS to learn. Political skills must be learned on the job. He developed the ability to work with others in situations that were not always clear or consistent with his values or his expectations. This area required compromises by WRS on a very frequent basis. He developed a negotiating technique of win/win for both parties. There were courses available to WRS to improve these negotiating skills. Developing these skills were very important (e.g., the Bosch negotiation). WRS's good negotiating skills, combined with good judgment, resulted in good political skills. This was very useful in his first managerial assignment when he was able to rally the support of his most troublesome subordinate and build trust as a new general manager with his staff (see discussions on pp. 40 and 62).

Interpreting body language helped WRS anticipate the outcomes of many situations. By anticipation, he was able to influence or modify outcomes if necessary. He frequently found people would tell him with their body language long before they verbalized their thoughts. He found in the Bosch negotiation, for example, that his opponents were constantly looking away from him after he gave a counterproposal. His opponents were visibly concerned as to how WRS would respond. WRS was able to adjust and influence his opponents' reaction.

WRS's academic background helped build his *analytical skills*. In corporate management, he found it to be difficult to do problem solving, to manage a large multi-functional organization, or to achieve a high-level management position without good analytical capabilities. Analytical skills allowed him to logically deduce conclusions from different and sometimes very meager facts. Many times he needed to understand, interpret, and use quantitative information. He found that analytical capabilities helped facilitate the deduction of answers and brought about better decisions.

Once WRS reached a goal, he found that remaining there is a continuous process. Succeeding in Corporate America is a full-time effort. Once one is at the top of an organization, continued success will depend on all of the ten items above as well as some role awareness. One fundamental mistake that managers make is not recognizing that they are also subordinates. The superordinate/subordinate combination for managers puts them in a double bind. They need to recognize that regardless of what position they have within the corporation, they are in a dual role—one as a superordinate and the other as a subordinate. Upon reflection on their role as a subordinate they may get important clues as to how their own subordinates may feel about their work environment. This empathy is oftentimes missing when the subordinate (manager) carries out his duties as a superordinate (manager).

The simple concept of foundation-building is not new and is oftentimes overlooked by the brightest of executives. Executives need to remember that they are the architects of their organizations. Architects would not think of designing or building a house without a solid foundation. Similarly, the design and building of an effective organization must include a solid foundation. Unlike the architect who relinquishes his work to a builder, an executive must implement his own designs. It is in the implementation that failure begins. In the haste of responding to the macro-driving forces of foreign competition, changing economic conditions, shareholder demands, and other pressures, some executives are foregoing the installation of a solid foundation to the organization.

To be sure, WRS's specialized knowledge and experience in the areas of finance, engineering, marketing, manufacturing, and human relations were as important to the building of his organization as materials are to the building of a house. In addition, the creation of a common culture is just as important to an organization as nails are to a house.

As WRS found out, the ultimate foundation of an organization rests in the deployment of human capital and not in its plant and equipment, technology, structure, processes, or financial systems. Moreover, human capital alone was not enough. WRS had to reduce uncertainty and dysfunctional conflict and build trust among the larger organizational reality and his subordinates to ensure a solid foundation. Similar to cement as a base which gives the foundation of a house strength, trust allowed his organization to remain strong during turbulent times.

In conclusion, trust is the basic foundation for an organization. It is hard to imagine how an organization can grow and prosper without trust. It should be viewed as a resource to the manager which, when developed, will foster teamwork, creativity, productivity, positive work environment, loyalty and commitment, ensuring improved company performance. A common source of mistrust lies in perception differences which exist among the work force and between the manager and the employees. This was clearly demonstrated in WRS's case. As the leader of the organization, he recognized that effective communication and consistent behavior on his part went a long way toward helping his employees have trust. He learned it must be earned and should not be taken for granted. Once WRS established it, it was cherished and replenished as an important foundation to him and his organization's integrity.

During his twenty-year corporate career, WRS developed a list of Do's and Don'ts which worked for him.

They are:

(1) Never play leapfrog with a unicorn. There are people in the work environment who present obstacles. They generally stand out among the crowd and should be obvious. They generally are a negative influence but do, in fact, have a lot of power within the organization. They may try to derail one's career. When one is in a situation where one is playing a tug-of-war with a "unicorn," one should be extremely careful. One should not leapfrog with one.

(2) Never burn a bridge, especially while standing on it. One will find the very bridge one burns may be needed to help one toward one's goal.

(3) There is a common expression spoken in Corporate America: "If one sees a snake, kill it." One should take caution. Friends and mentors do not always appear in their expected "forms." So if one sees an individual whom one clearly can classify as a "snake," remember one could be killing a relationship with someone who could be a future mentor.

(4) One will encounter a chameleon. One may become a chameleon. Adoption of a chameleon type of personality can be used as an excellent defense or offense if done skillfully. One should be encouraged to reflect on one's abilities in this area because when under attack, one may have to change one's position frequently.

(5) One should never draw a line in the sand. It is important during negotiations to create a climate of win/win and leave options for the other person to win and to gracefully change their position when needed. There may be a better compromise further along in the discussion.

(6) One should work hard. One should remain dedicated and work long productive hours. The dictionary is the only place where "success" comes before "work."

(7) Do network. It is important to network and develop friends and allies throughout the company as well as the social community. Maintain these connections. One never knows who will throw a lifeline to save one in a certain situation or tell one about an opportunity.

(8) Develop a sense of humbleness. There are times in one's career where one is faced with situations which will not be going one's way or where one must grin and bear. Humbleness is the key. One must have it as part of one's inventory of actions and employ when necessary.

(9) Don't take recognition for granted. American management has a ways to go before this is a natural behavior.

(10) If one is going to play politics in the corporate world, one should become the best at it. A mediocre politician in political life does not get elected for a second term. In Corporate America they are set aside.

(11) They tell boxers when they get in the ring, "protect yourself at all times." One should carry this thought along as one progresses.

(12) One's socializing in the office or the appearance of it can be professionally dangerous. Whether one's actions are real or perceived to be true, the results could be the same.

(13) One should be cautious not to express political or religious views in a way where one takes a controversial or uncompromising stance. One may not know the position of a given discussant or whether they agree or disagree or the influence they may have on one's future.

WRS found many times where proper attention to one of the above do's or don'ts helped him to cope in problem situations.

There are different ways of characterizing the corporate environment. Some were described above, including making certain one has the proper education commensurate with one's career goals, acquires the right experiences, develops good personality traits, polishes one's professional interactions and one's dress and appearance, develops patience, develops a good career plan, is flexible, and does the needed networking.

NOTE

1. The Equal Employment Opportunity (EEO) Act in 1964 accelerated the rate of change in work force diversity. A Diverse Work Force (DWF) is the sum of differences in a working community by gender, age, and ethnic origin.

Chapter 7

Corporate Dilemma; Implications; Conclusion

Corporate Dilemma

Companies which, during the 1970s, embarked on aggressive recruiting efforts and hired a lot of Blacks, are finding that very few have made it to the top of the organization. This is rekindling the concerns of bias in decision-making and other discriminatory practices. An increased number of minorities are leaving companies where these feelings exist. One company president asked a team of executives to investigate this problem within his organization and was surprised at the findings. The executives found that the reason very few minorities had made it to higher levels of management was a result of what they called "blocking and tackling" of Blacks at the lower and middle levels of the organization. The model the author developed to describe this is shown in Figure 5.

The circles shown in the vice president category represent WRS and two other vice presidents. They were also part of the executive team. The company has 75,000 employees of which 4% are Black. The above scenario describes the situation where many Black professionals are concentrated at the bottom of the organization. There is a

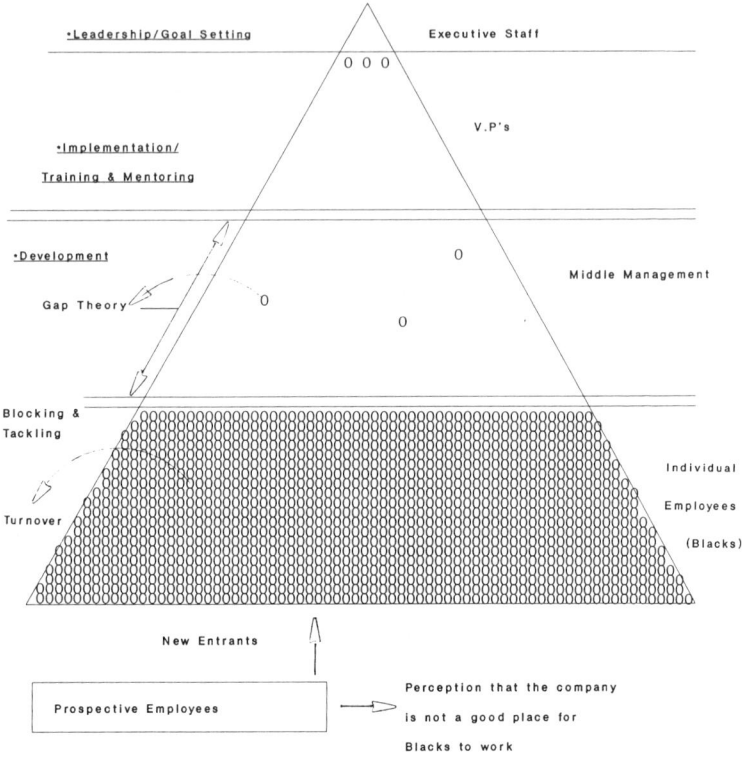

Figure 5

gap to develop those who survive blocking and tackling and make it up into middle management. White managers who are not sensitive to the racial differences while managing Blacks are creating racial tension in the work environment. They are not providing Blacks the opportunity to develop in order to become part of the lasting and useful management team. This, in many cases, is a purposeful strategy on their part. Blacks are seeing this as racism. They become disgruntled and leave the company. WRS left his first company for this reason.

Furthermore, this situation makes it difficult for the company to hire Blacks. Without visible signs within the company that Blacks can advance their careers, potential recruits develop a perception that the company is not a good place for Blacks to work. This creates a dilemma. Blacks are leaving the company at a faster rate than they are being replaced, so the company is losing very valuable talent. In addition, as the population of Blacks dwindles, those who are less mobile become less productive as does the work environment. Blacks become preoccupied with job security concerns and the negative job atmosphere. This image begins to build on itself causing a gap to form in the middle of the organization. This scenario, if allowed to persist, will degrade the financial performance of the company.

The Black executives at the top of the organization are in the best position to describe what is affecting Blacks and what they have to do to advance through the gap. The causes of the repressive outcomes are being addressed, little by little. Company leaders do not take advantage of the knowledge and experience of the Blacks who have managed to cope. The president whose company could be described by the model in Figure 5 was concerned enough to listen. This case study describes similar incidents that affected WRS.

In *Time* magazine (August 7, 1989), an article "Unfinished Business," indicated: "A sweeping survey of race relations [A Common Destiny] finds that black progress has stalled because of a stagnant economy and white resistance to equality." In this article numerous references were made to the just released report, "A Common Destiny," which dispelled a number of myths concerning statements about racial progress. One of the myths says "overt discrimination has virtually vanished in the past twenty years."

Also indicated was the following:

> As "A Common Destiny" makes clear, a considerable amount of remaining black-white inequality is due to continuing discriminatory treatment of blacks. The earliest evidence is in housing. Since the 1960's there has been almost no measurable progress in housing integration. In 1980 in the sixteen metropolitan areas with the largest black population, was rated 80 on a 0–100 scale on which 100 meant total segregation. These discriminatory patterns cannot be explained only by black-white economic differences (p. 6).

It is evident that Black progress toward equality and changing White attitudes and behaviors will take a long time and will continue to be an uphill battle for Blacks.

Racism in society does make a difference in Black attainment. The power of the majority, the prejudice and discrimination that ensues, the lack of economic balance, and the inability to bring about radical change will continue to play a significant role in the values, beliefs, attitudes, and behavior of the Black American. In the words of Dr. Martin Luther King, Jr.: "I have a dream that my four little children will one day live in a nation where they will not be judged by the color of their skin but by the content of their character." Until then Black development will continue to be influenced by racism. The practice of racism will continue to plague Corporate America's progress. This remains one of Corporate America's biggest dilemmas. The changing demographics (see Appendix B) will continue to exacerbate the dilemma and force solutions. The solutions will not be cost-free in the short run, but gains will be great in the longer run.

Implications:

Since a significant infusion of training will be required for White male managers who manage Black subordinates, it is important to note some of the current concerns expressed by Blacks in the literature (See Appendix A). As Black professionals look around today in Corporate America, they find it very difficult to locate role models to give them hope for career advancement. Their frustration is with the speed of acceptance and how they can explain to their White superiors why their behavior is what it is (impatience, lack of trust or understanding).

As the number of Black professionals increases, the literature has shown there will be an increase in the tension and concern of Whites. If the failure to provide upward mobility for Blacks continues, there will be rising discontent in the work environment. The consequences of this double bind will include lower productivity, higher absenteeism, and turnover among Black professionals. The Black professional can favorably influence the assimilation process by enhancing one's abilities to adapt to the work environment. This would include:

(1) Career Planning—develop a road map of the position desired and the strategy to achieve it;
(2) Networking—develop a broad base of people in positions of influence who can help;
(3) Communication Skills—develop exceptional skills in listening, speaking, and so forth;
(4) Education—education is a continuing process to be kept constant.

Employers' affirmative action programs, improving equality, training and skill building of managers, and self development will be occurring simultaneously in the work environment. The future will continue to represent a significant challenge for Black professionals as job opportunities expand. Wilson's (1980) observation that race is declining in significance is not confirmed by most of the literature, and so it should continue to be tested skeptically in the corporate setting.

The traditional training of White male managers needs to be updated to incorporate this new mix of employee population. The traditional methods of training and executive skill-building are no longer adequate to deal with continued diversification in the employee population. The increasing percentage of Black professionals in the workplace, for example, has created a renewed awareness among Whites of the past discrimination practices. The following is a summary of the actions required:

(1) Corporate America should increase its investment in cultural awareness programs, conflict management training, and other skill-building programs to facilitate the assimilation of Black professionals. Companies should enforce affirmative action initiatives to ensure minorities equal opportunity for advancement, encourage the mentoring process to provide role models, and provide counselors to help facilitate the process of mobility.

(2) White managers should expand their knowledge of the cultural differences which exist and seek to expand their skills. They should develop an understanding of how their biases influence their decisions and seek ways to eliminate or minimize their impact. They should foster an environment which would breed trust, under-

standing and empowerment for all employees.

(3) White professional employees should, similar to the White manager, become more aware of how biases influence the socialization process, trust, and the fostering of teamwork. Every attempt should be made to eliminate or minimize the racial biases.

(4) Black professional employees should also look inward to remove their racial biases. The road to success in Corporate America will require the continued endurance Blacks have demonstrated for generations. Similar to the challenges faced through years of slavery, riots, and segregation, assimilation into Corporate America will also bring new challenges. How prejudice and discrimination are practiced may not be as obvious inside a Corporation as outside it.

The growth in the labor market will create new opportunities for Black professionals. As these opportunities are realized and the number of Blacks increases, history has shown, an increase in tension and conflict with Whites occurs. Tension and conflict, among the employee population, will bring a decrease in companies' financial performance. Corporate America should increase and expand investments in training and skill building for White managers and professional employees. The training should include cultural awareness, conflict resolution, and other programs to help remove bias from decision-making influenced by race and ethnicity. This should facilitate the assimilation process, provide a good return on investment, and allow Corporate America to remain in a position of primacy.

Conclusion

Blacks have shown continued endurance for over 300

years. Without economic power or influence, and with only the appeal to the moralism of the broader White society, the chances of bringing about radical change is slim. Although gains have been made in the areas of education, economics, and job status, the relative position of Blacks to Whites is stagnant. (See Appendix C.)

This was a case study of a Black American male and the trials and tribulations he experienced during his quest toward becoming a successful professional in America. The significant periods of this case study were: The Early Years (1951–1957); The Self-Preparation (1958–1969); and finally, The Journey through Corporate America (1970–1990). Each period contributed a significant part to WRS's case. During 1951–1957, he attended grade school while growing up in a ghetto. WRS began, during this period, to know what it is like to experience discrimination. The segregationist policies of the South made him aware of his color. The discrimination practices of Whites were designed to make Blacks feel inferior. He also established a strong desire to somehow overcome this inhumane treatment he and his family received. During the period 1958–1969, a growing maturity revealed the realism of his challenge. He began to crystallize the difficulty he faced in order to overcome the obstacles along his path. His education helped him obtain a more mature vision of what needed to be done and the understanding needed to begin. He became convinced that a good education, the right work experience, and careful planning were essential ingredients. He graduated from high school with good grades and a four-year scholarship. Although his college education enabled him to overcome some economic pain and suffering, he found a new form of racism in the corporate society.

Finally, the period between 1970–1990 marks the time during which the corporate journey was begun and success achieved. This period is analogous to the crossing of a minefield without having knowledge of where the mines were located. The heightened awareness of the impact of taking an incorrect step was very keen—the disastrous consequences to his success. The difficulty he experienced in assimilating into Corporate America continued to mature him. He learned how to: improve his leadership style, exercise political behavior, manage racism, be patient, manage conflict, build trust, and lead a large organization. Even more important, he learned how to create win/win scenarios.

The important lessons learned are then summarized. The lessons should be useful to the reader who desires to use this case study as a model for his or her corporate strategy. Included was a discussion of the implications of the growing number of Blacks in the work environment to Corporate America. With the growing number of Blacks in the professional work environment, the implications to the various stakeholders involved were also discussed. This case study formed the basis for the implications. It is concluded that evidence exists in which racism did and will continue to influence the success of Black professionals along their journey in Corporate America. Something more must be done.

APPENDIXES

Appendix A

A Literature Review

There is evidence that racism does exist in society (Thurow, 1969; Becker, 1971: Campbell, 1971; Schiller, 1984; Schuman, Steeh, and Bobo, 1985). Corporate America is a microcosm of our society. White managers' behavior in the corporate environment is indicative of symbolic racism (Kinder, 1986). In some cases this may be in the form of tokenism (Bowser, 1985). In any event there is clear evidence that inequality does exist (Work, 1984; Sniderman and Hagen, 1985). Certain authors do indicate that better supervision is needed for Blacks (Murphy, 1973). The present supervision is showing signs of racial discrimination (Brown and Ford, Jr., 1977; Fernandez, 1985; Anderson, 1978). This form of discrimination is leading to perception differences between the White supervisor and the Black subordinate (Alderfer, Alderfer, Tucker, and Tucker, 1980). There is clear evidence that discrimination is resulting in non-parity of Black professionals in all levels within the corporate hierarchy (Semyonov, Hoyt, and Scott, 1984). Black professional non-parity is a consequence of the barriers confronting them in their career advancement (Wells, Jr. and Jennings, 1984; Dickens and Dickens, 1982). The literature provides case studies which give clear accounts of individuals who actually experienced bias in the work environment (Jones, Jr., 1973; Davis and Watson, 1985). A high percentage of Blacks in the corporate setting are feeling alienated and perceive a lack of job power (Nixon, 1980). These authors' observations support the belief that there is a difference in managerial behaviors of White managers toward Blacks, which are race-related and not work-related.

The changing demographics of more Blacks in career jobs in the work force will have far-reaching implications on the present and future decision-making of managers. It is concluded, based on the literature and related research, that ethnicity is a factor in decision making. This leads to a need to prepare managers for the steady work force diversification. Recognizing that the rising diversity in the corporate environment is bringing new challenges—to train managers to keep all productivity high with minimum impact on financial performance has a higher priority today in Corporate America than in any previous period. Since the White male manager and Black professional subordinate relationship is increasing in occurrence, it can be used as a model to establish a broader application of diverse work force training for managers. This study revealed some of the potential perceptual differences existing between White managers with Black subordinates and implications to training programs. It also focused on key managerial behaviors, as these authors did.

Appendix B

Blacks and Whites in Management Groups

The Changing Demographics

The changing demographics of more women and minorities in the work force will have far-reaching implications on the present and future decision-making of business leaders. The Human Resource Department, for example, continues to be challenged with determining the most effective development programs for culturally mixed work environments, child care for the offspring of working parents, and unmet needs for minority groups. As Cravens, Hills, and Woodruff (1976) state: "The social environment affects the functioning of virtually everything in a democratic society and implicitly sets the priorities as well as the direction for change" (p. 76). The influence of society is felt in all aspects of the macro-environment, internal and external.

As stated earlier, the driving forces of the future in U.S. industry are the growing influence of technology, information exchange, foreign competition and demographics. Until recently, demographics has not received as much attention as some of the others.

Johnston and Packer, in the book *Workforce 2000: Work and Workers for the Twenty-First Century*, stated the following:

Minorities Will Be a Growing Share of the Workforce

Over the next 13 years, blacks, Hispanics, and other minorities will make up a large share of the expansion of the labor force. Non-whites, for example, will comprise 29 percent of the net additions to the workforce between 1985 and 2000 and then will constitute more than 15 percent of the workforce in the year 2000 (p. 89).

More statistics appear from the Bureau of Labor Statistics:

Table 1
NON-WHITES ARE A GROWING SHARE
OF THE WORKFORCE
(numbers in millions)

	1970	1985	2000
Working Age Population (16+)	137.1	184.1	213.7
Non-White Share	10.9%	13.6%	15.7%
Labor Force	82.8	115.5	140.4
Non-White Share	11.1%	13.1%	15.5%
Labor Force Increase (Over Previous Period)	X	32.7	25.0
Non-White Share	X	8.4%	29.0%

Source: Bureau of Labor Statistics, *Handbook of Labor Statistics, 1985*, Tables 4 and 5; and Hudson Institute.

These statistics will require a more serious look to see implications for employee training programs, managerial development, conflict resolution alternatives, absenteeism, turnover, productivity and many other issues.

Appendix C

Black Progress

The results of Black achievement in society can be summarized using demographic measures. Farley (1984) divided Black progress into three areas: (1) measurements which clearly show the status of Blacks relative to Whites is improving, (2) those which show no improvement, and (3) those which are mixed.

Improving

He points out that racial differences in educational obtainment are certainly decreasing. On the eve of World War II, adult Blacks averaged about three fewer years of schooling than Whites, but by the early 1980's, the racial difference declined to one and a half years. In addition, secondary school attendance converged, and by mid-1970's racial differences in enrollment through age 17 had about disappeared. Despite the obvious progress for Blacks, he cautions, there is still a substantial difference in attainment. Among those who were in their early twenties in 1980, about 85% of the Whites but only 70% of the Blacks had finished high school. Among those in their late twenties, about one White in four, but one Black in eight, had four or more years of college (U.S. Bureau of the Census, 1980, Table 1).

Racial progress, Farley observed, was also evident in the occupations of employed workers. Among Blacks the white collar positions had gone up rapidly. Back in 1960, the 10% of all workers who were Black held only 3% of the professional and management jobs. In 1980, Blacks still made up about 10% of the work force, but they held 6% of the managerial and professional jobs (U.S. Bureau of Labor Statistics, 1979, Table 18;1983, Tables 23 and 48).

The final area of improvement was in the earnings of employed workers. In 1959, Black men earned only 61% as much per hour as White men; twenty years later they earn 74% as much. The racial gap in earnings for women, however, had all but disappeared. In 1959, Black women earned only 61% as much per hour as White women; by 1979 they earned 98% as much. This discrepancy between the wages paid to similar workers of different races he called "the cost of being Black," and it is one estimate of the cost of discrimination.

No Improvement

Farley's (1984) analysis showed that the level of unemployment had no improvement. Blacks were as far behind in 1979 as in 1959. The unemployment rate of Black men was twice that of White men in the mid-1950's, he states, and the ratio has changed little since then. In the 70's, he noted, the proportion of men aged 25 to 54 who were not in the labor force rose from 8% to 13% for non-Whites, from 3% to 5% for Whites.

Mixed

The indicators which are mixed include integration of schools, the incomes of families, property and residential segregation. In most rural areas of the South, Farley (1984) points out, the promise of the Brown decision has largely been achieved and Black and White children now attend the same schools. But little progress has been made in integrating public schools in the nation's largest metropolises. The incomes of Black families in 1982 were only 55% of Whites vs. 52% of median incomes of Whites in 1959. In 1959, 55% of the Black population lived in households whose cash income fell below the poverty line; in 1970, it was only 34%. Poverty, he states, has become more commonplace among both races since 1979; 36% of the Black population fell below poverty line by 1982. Farley (1984) also indicated that residential segregation of Blacks from Whites may also be a mixed indicator revealing progress in some locations and no change in others. The Civil Rights Act of 1968 banned discrimination in the sale or rental of housing, and the incomes of Black husband/wife family rose more rapidly in the 70's than those of similar White families. These changes, he notes, along with the continued liberalization of White attitudes, may have made it easier for Blacks to enter formerly White neighborhoods. Farley (1984) concludes with the view that Black gains are widespread and significant, but many more decades of change similar to the 60's and 70's will be necessary to eradicate differences due to race.

1989 Report

In *Time* magazine (August 7, 1989) an article "Unfinished Business," indicated: "A sweeping survey of race relations [A Common Destiny] finds that black progress has stalled because of a stagnant economy and white resistance to equality." In this article numerous references were made to the just released report, "A Common Destiny," which dispelled a number of myths concerning statements about racial progress. One of the myths says, "overt discrimination has virtually vanished in the past 20 years." Also indicated was the following:

As "A Common Destiny" makes clear a considerable amount of remaining black-white inequality is due to continuing discriminatory treatment of blacks. The earliest evidence is in housing. Since the 1960's there has been almost no measurable progress in housing integration. In 1980 in the sixteen metropolitan areas with the largest black population, was rated 80 on a 0–100 scale on which 100 meant total segregation. These discriminatory patterns cannot be explained only by black-white economic differences (p. 6).

It is evident that Black progress toward equality and changing White attitudes and behaviors will take a long time and will continue to be an uphill battle for Blacks.

Appendix D

Networking: Self-help in Assimilating into Corporate America

Introduction

There has been substantial increase in the number of Blacks and minorities entering Corporate America over the past twenty years. This large influx will be the next major challenge for Corporate America. The challenge is greater because of the greater diversity of the employee population. As the number of minorities increase, it will lead to increased resistance towards acceptance by the larger White employee population. Specifically, the White/Black relationship has historically been strained due to, among other things, the different perception each has of the other's intention. Kochman (1981) states: "Black and white culture differences are generally ignored when attempts are made to understand how and why black and white communications fail" (p. 7).

The Civil Rights Act 1964 and the following Affirmative Action initiatives have and will continue to influence the growth of opportunities for advancement of Blacks and other minorities. Corporations are responding with cultural awareness programs and other development activities for middle and upper management. The rate of these changes is slower than the influx of minorities into the work force.

While the corporations are responding at the rate they are, Blacks and other minorities must develop their own techniques to accelerate their advancement up the corporate ladder. As minorities accumulate at the lower levels, a key tactic to begin advancing their career ahead of the corporate programs is to utilize the technique of networking. As long as prejudice and discrimination prevail in the corporate setting, Blacks will have to continue to employ as many techniques as possible to advance themselves. Networking should provide Blacks with an infrastructure of supporters within the corporation which will allow them to advance at a much faster rate.

Importance

A common technique, frequently used to advance to the top in Corporate America, has been networking. Networking is an important strategy of human development. In order to succeed in Corporate America, you need to establish influential sponsors throughout an organization. Your value as perceived by others in the corporation is a very important asset. Education, job performance, unity through group representation, are all important; however, networking with a broad group of people can enhance Blacks and other minorities' ability to overcome many of the challenges they face in advancing their careers. The following summarizes the overall assimilation strategy, an important ingredient of building relationships:

No One Is an Island

No one is an island, everyone needs to be wanted.
To be wanted, you must be known;
To be known, you must build relationships;
To build relationships, you must communicate;
To communicate, you must have something to say;
To have something to say, you must have a plan;
To have a plan, you must know where you are going;
To know where you are going, you must know where you
    are;
To know where you are, you must know who you are;
To know who you are is the beginning.

Networking is a very important tactic for Blacks to employ in order to succeed in Corporate America. The concept of networking is tied closely to the phrase "it's not what you know, but whom you know." In Corporate America the phrase takes on a new meaning for minorities—it is a combination of the "who" and the "what" which is needed to get ahead.

Basic Definition

Networking is creating friends and allies, people who are in positions to recruit, clear paths, provide a reference, or who could provide guidance for professionals to get ahead and to obtain their career goals. The focus should be with people in positions of influence. Networking is more difficult for Blacks, especially in corporations. The long history of subordination, unequal treatment, and discrimination employed against them has contributed to many of the perception differences discussed earlier. This makes it more difficult for Blacks to be assertive and establish broader networks of high level executives within an organization. Generally these higher level people are White and have the perceptions that were discussed earlier that impede authentic relationships between them. With these thoughts in mind, Blacks tend not to establish a relationship that will allow for them to be counseled. Generally, Blacks feel because they have struggled to get where they are, they do not need additional help (and therefore do not develop the talent to network) to continue up the corporate ladder. As a result, many minorities remain at the entry level in their professions.

Ease

Networking is a natural process. As young adults, one's network included teachers, parents, relatives, friends, and other people with whom one had something in common, members of fraternities, councils, and so forth. As one matured, one's network expanded to include work professionals and other people in the community. Even if one did not do so young in life, building a network is a natural act in the maturing process. In the corporate environment, however, it is not always so easy.

Why

The reason why Blacks need to network is that it allows for them to tap into a source of knowledge about many people in their organization and outside it. Skillful networking would include only productive, successful, and emotionally positive associates. People who are well respected and have demonstrated success in their own careers are the ones to network with. When interacting in a networking fashion, focus on pertinent and useful information. You should engage in a fair exchange of contructive ideas. The information exchanged should be useful for both parties. This statement is probably the most important principle Blacks can learn in the corporate environment. Following this thought can provide a perspective to understanding how the corporate environment functions.

Prerequisites

Networking is an art and one should satisfy certain prerequisites before one begins. These include making certain one's education is appropriate for one's career goals, being an excellent performer, and having good personal traits (such as communication skills, listening skills, and so forth). In addition, one should identify the desired next assignment and begin to identify the people who are needed to help you achieve your goal. These few preliminary prerequisites should allow for one to respond to questions while engaging in the area of networking with higher level executives.

Where?

Knowing where to network is also very important. One should carefully think through where one plans to increase one's experience. Networking should be concentrated in an area where one would pursue one's next assignment. One should not limit oneself, however, to only one area because of constant movement of people from company to company. Opportunities to advance may occur outside of one's company or area.

How?

The following is an approach to networking from Germann, Blumenson, and Arnold's book entitled *Working and Liking It*, in which they state:

(1) Make a list of all the people who are in key positions in the company whom you know well and with whom you enjoy free and open communications. There may only be one or two people on this list. That is okay; it is a start.

(2) Add to this list the names of all the people in the responsible key positions whom you know slightly but would like to build a better or closer working relationship with.

(3) Now add the people whom you consider essential to your network but with whom you are not acquainted or with whom you haven't communicated in the past beyond minimum daily courtesy (New York: Ballantine Books, 1984).

Again, note people in a decision-making position and give them priority, while remembering peers and people below one's level who can also be important sources of information about unfamiliar areas of the organization.

Appendix E

Valuing and Managing Diversity: The Trust Factor

Introduction

A vital element needed in organizations to enable them to remain effective and overcome size, tribal warfare, cultural diversity, and changing environmental influences is organizational trust. An executive's challenge is to build an organization that he or she can be proud of. Some executives have attempted to manage by the numbers for short term results, while others have looked beyond the short term to a longer term approach using strategic planning. In the latter case, they typically develop faith in a vision that may require trading off short term results for what they believe will return long term gains. Although there are different approaches to building effective organizations, none will be as long lasting as the one where the executive first builds and then maintains a strong foundation of trust.

Trust and Trust Equity

The dictionary defines "trust" as a firm belief or confidence in the honesty, integrity, reliability, justice, etc., of another person or thing; faith; reliance. Have we matured in a society which has biased us as adults to begin our relationships with a low level of trust? Is it human nature to be skeptical? Leaders should not assume that trust will automatically be extended when they enter into a new relationship with subordinates, peers, or superiors.

The notion of trust can be described graphically borrowing from a mathematical term—Asymptotic Curve. This is shown in Figure 6 using what the author describes as an asymptotic trust curve.

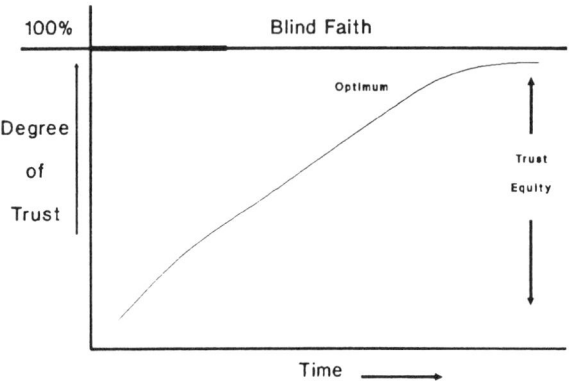

Figure 6 Asymptotic "Trust" Curve

The theory illustrated in the above chart is that relationships over time never reach the point of blind faith (100% trusting). As relationships mature over time, a trust equity is built up in the relationship. Familiarity between the parties grows in such a way that the parties eventually reach an "optimum" level of trust (and hence an optimum level of uncertainty between them). The reason this is referred to as "optimum" is because seldom can one support the claim of having blind faith (100% trusting) in another for all situations. An element of doubt will always exist. Managers who have the immediate expectation from employees of 100%

trust may be disappointed. They should focus on building trust equity over a period of time and try to reach some optimum level. The optimum level will be contingent upon the parties involved (e.g., their relationship in the organization, frequency of their contact, importance of the issues involved, their personality type, and their need for control). Employees in the organization are at a different point along the curve with their manager, their peers, their work environment, and their social environment.

Moving up the continuum toward 100% trust, does require that employees have positive relationship encounters. Graphically, this is shown in Figure 7.

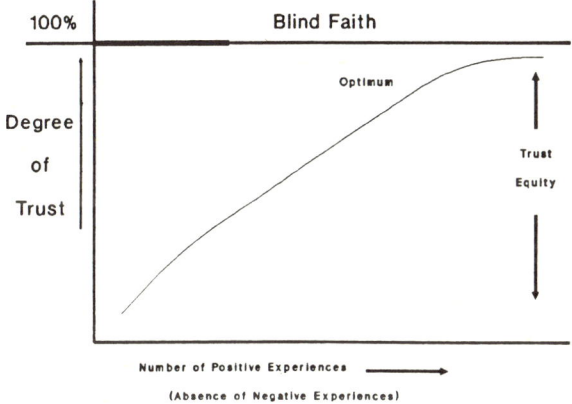

Figure 7 Asymptotic "Trust" Curve

A continuation of positive experiences will build trust equity and hence, a trusting relationship.

To be sure, moving up the curve will not be easy. Each time the expectations of the other are violated it will bring a degree of uncertainty back into the relationship. This new uncertainty reduces the equity buildup and moves the parties back down the curve.

Trust is a very fragile, sensitive feeling that must be

earned in a relationship in a continuous process. It's such a vital element to maintaining a positive relationship (with minimum uncertainty), leaders should be highly motivated and preoccupied with obtaining trust equity across their entire organization. A little trust can be leveraged so highly that many leaders will employ political behavior just to obtain a little.

One characteristic of trust deserves specific attention. Trust is also so volatile that misunderstanding resulting from perception differences can serve to reverse totally whatever trust equity is accrued. In human affairs we defend ourselves against this. Prenuptial agreements or golden parachutes are few examples of approaches used as a contingent against a loss of trust equity in relationships.

Therefore, the manager must continually add trust equity: banking it is not reliable. A theoretical extension to the asymptotic trust theory is shown in Figure 8. This is where, at the beginning of a relationship, trust is extended as a given. This is presented as theoretical because some would argue that at the beginning of the relationship one would not have a reason not to trust the relationship.

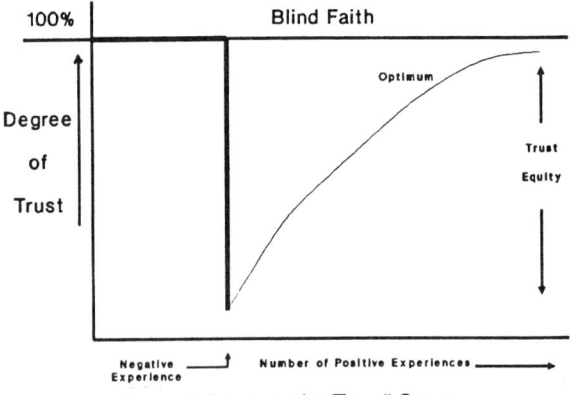

Figure 8 Asymptotic "Trust" Curve

The above graph can be referred to as the "no one is perfect" scenario. This states that if one exhibits blind trust at the beginning of a relationship, it's just a matter of time when it will change to the asymptotic curve discussed earlier, thereby proving that no one is perfect.

As the changing macro environmental influences flow into the work environment, they will add to the uncertainty that already exists. The uncertainty has an "*untrusting*" flavor to it. The lack of trust breeds uncertainty, uncertainty breeds conflict, and if the conflict is dysfunctional, it will certainly have an impact on the organizational effectiveness.

A Conceptual Model:

A breakdown of trust within the organization (specifically between the manager and subordinate) will necessitate conflict resolution alternatives for employees. Figure 9 is the author's model which conceptualizes the situation for use in the case of workforce diversification:

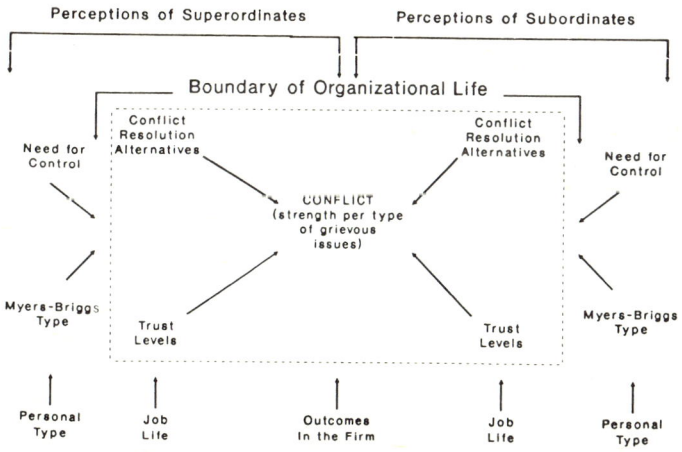

Figure 9 Model for Work Force Diversification

111

The above model shows conflict (the strength of grievous issues representing tension-related behavior) as the center of employee organizational life. Leadership style and the need for control are important variables operating on how each (superordinate and subordinate) perceives one's work environment and how one responds to conflict. It is expected that if managers are not able to resolve the conflicts resulting from the different employee expectations, it will result in negative impact upon the work environment.

The leader is in a double bind. If the minority employee does not have options and his manager exerts certain power over him, he will become disgruntled and low morale and low productivity may result. On the other hand, if the employee does have alternatives within or outside the work environment, his manager's power is severely reduced. This can be perceived on the part of the manager as a loss of control of the situation. This latter case is also not good. It is hard to predict managerial behavior if the manager senses a loss of power control over the situation with the employees. Majority managers might introduce bias in their decision-making as it relates to minority employees. This can be done through selection of job assignments, performance appraisals, and other subtle covert behavior.

Racial Conflicts

A good example of the above is the race relation between Whites and non-Whites. It has historically been strained both in the community and in the work environment. Much has been written which attempts to explain the source of this tension. Differences in values, attitudes, personality, perceptions and education have been at the heart of most accepted explanations. If the White male manager's frame of reference is different from his professional non-White or female subordinate's, what implications does this have on his ability to manage? To lead? All too often productivity in corporate America has been lost because problem solving has focused on the "person" and not on the "problem." If differences in the frame of reference of the White to non-White or male to female relationships do exist, maybe it is explainable why the "person" focus rather than the "problem" focus may occur more often than in White to White, non-White to non-White, or female to female manager-subordinate relationships.

If a manager or subordinate wants to get one's way in a given situation, each must have or develop a *position of strength* over the other. This *position of strength* is the source of power to be used to exert influence over the other. A manager typically has *position power* over his subordinates. A subordinate is faced with either developing a *critical skill (knowledge power)* or becoming a powerful *informal leader* within the organization. In either case, it makes him essential to the success of the manager or company. If one has a greater power over the other, it will become a potential source of conflict. Trust existing between the two will keep the power advantage in balance.

Appendix F

WRS's Resume

<u>Career Objective</u>	General management—having profit and loss responsibility while operating a competitive electronic oriented business.
<u>Education</u>	B. S. Physics, Duquesne University ('68), Pittsburgh, PA M. S. Physics, Indiana University ('69), Indiana, PA. Ph.D. Administration/Management, Walden University ('90), Minneapolis, MN, Dissertation Title: *Case Study of Work Force Diversification: An Introspection Into Managerial Behavior.*
<u>Summary of Experience</u>	All of my professional career involved high volume, high technology, electronic oriented products (customized and standard) where high market growth, numerous competitors (especially foreign) were involved. Twenty years professional experience within two major corporations: Honeywell (12 years), and General Electric (8.5 years).

Seventeen years of progressive managerial assignments: three years as General Manager, nine years in Engineering and Manufacturing, eight years in Marketing and Strategic Planning.

9/87–4/91 **Honeywell, Keyboard Division, Vice President and General Manager**

This position reports to the President, Industrial Automation and Controls. This worldwide P & L responsibility includes all business functions in a division which is autonomous. The Keyboard Division is responsible for the design, manufacturing, and marketing for Operator Interface products to the Computer/Business Equipment, Industrial and Commercial markets worldwide. The Division has five locations: Freeport, IL; Las Cruces, NM; Juarez, Mexico; El Paso, TX (Headquarters); El Paso, TX (Warehouse); and 1500 employees. Significant growth in orders, revenue, and profit occurred over this period including new product introductions and profit turnaround. A prestigious "Excellence Award" was given to the Division by the Honeywell Chairman and CEO for performance.

7/85–9/87	**Honeywell, Micro Switch Division, Director of Operations** This position reported to the Vice President & Unit Director. This P & L responsibility covers Engineering, Manufacturing, Quality, Production Control and Product Marketing for keyboard and touch panel products. Three manufacturing plants, including Freeport, IL; Las Cruces, NM; and Juarez, Mexico; as well as engineering and marketing functions headquartered in El Paso, TX, encompassing over 1,000 employees. Significant new product developments, cost reductions, and quality improvements were accomplished during this period.
11/82–7/85	**Honeywell, Micro Switch Division, Director of Engineering** This position reported to the Vice President & Unit Director. This engineering responsibility covers a broad range of switches, keyboards, integrated circuit design and CAD/CAM. I directed the overall design, development, and introduction of new products; and directed the necessary design improvement and modification of the existing products to be in concert with Marketing, Production and Operating plans. The resolution of major technical problems with the existing

product offerings and the design and release of replacement products (including the Silent Tactile Keyboard) was accomplished during this period.

1/81–11/82   Honeywell, Micro Switch Division, Director of Marketing

This position reported to the Vice President & Unit Director. This marketing responsibility covers a broad range of switches, keyboards and components. I developed and executed short and long range strategies, annual marketing and product development programs, product line sales and profitability; sales promotions and direct sale supports on major projects on a worldwide basis. Major new product introductions, pricing strategies and strategic direction of the business were set during this period.

5/80–1/81   Honeywell, Micro Switch Division, Director of Market Planning

This position reported to the Vice President of Marketing. This strategic planning responsibility required the development of long range divisional plans in the Computer and Business Equipment, Commercial, Automotive, Consumer, and Aerospace Ordinance and Marine (ATOM) markets. The

1981 divisional market plans were published and provided strategic direction to the operating units.

7/78–5/80

Honeywell, Micro Switch Division, Marketing Manager, Solid State Components Group

I was responsible for managing the overall business activities for the Division's Solid State Sensor products. Specifically, this includes products based on Hall and Piezoresistive technologies. This responsibility includes pricing, product definition, short and long range planning, giving engineering and manufacturing direction for all product areas. Extensive training of the selling organization in Solid State Sensor technology was accomplished. Liaison with the Optoelectronic Division was required in order to coordinate and integrate the marketing of the sensor products of both divisions.

2/76–7/78

General Electric Company, Semiconductor Products Department Marketing Manager—Signal Products

I was responsible for managing the overall business activities for worldwide marketing of twelve profit centers. This included such products as power transistors, signal diodes and transistors, inverter power devices and optoelectronic devices. Specifically, this P & L responsibility included pricing, short and long range planning, product definition and engineering, and manufacturing direction for all profit centers. Over twenty-five percent travel required.

3/73–2/76	**General Electric Company, Semiconductor Products Department Manager Product Planning**

This responsibility included various advance planning assignments for the following product areas: low current rectifiers, silicon signal and power transistors, germanium transistors and diodes, power modules, selenium thyrectors and optoelectronics products. This marketing assignment required over forty percent worldwide travel. I have traveled throughout the United States and Europe developing accounts and negotiating contracts.

10/71–3/73	**General Electric Company, Semiconductor Products Department Technical Manager/Project Engineer**

I was responsible for production, process and quality control, design and packaging of all optoelectronic product including solid state relays. I provided technical direction to a staff of engineers. I have developed low-cost packaging techniques for optical couplers. In mid 1972, I traveled to Japan and Seoul, South Korea, to teach and train foreign engineers techniques for utilizing a patented process for assembling optoelectronic devices. I have set up high-volume manufacturing facilities in the Far East. In late 1972, I developed and introduced to the electronic market General Electric's first solid state optoelectronic relay.

7/70–10/71	General Electric Company, Semiconductor Products Department Advance Design Engineer

Responsible for assessing the application of semiconductor as sensors material with emphasis on temperature, magnetic, optoelectronic, and current sensors for appliance and industrial needs. I have designed, fabricated, packaged and evaluated temperature, magnetic and optoelectronic sensors made from silicon. I have filed three patent dockets on process for making sensor devices.

9/69–6/70	Bryn Mawr College, Bryn Mawr, PA, Department of Physics, Physics Lab Instructor
8/68–8/69	Indiana University of PA, Indiana, PA, Department of Physics, Physics Lab Instructor

Community & Other Activities	Board Member—Computer and Business Equipment Manufacturers Association
	Board Member—Family Life Center, 1983–85
	Young Executive Council—State Bank of Freeport, Freeport, IL
	Chairperson—Micro Switch's Technology Council, 1983–84
	Committee Member—Honeywell's H. W. Sweatt Awards
	Commissioner—Water & Sewer Department of Freeport, Freeport, IL
	Consultant—NAACP of Freeport
	Member—Physics Honor Society
Key Company Courses	Management Development Course
	Workshop in Negotiating Skills
	Economic Analysis of Alternatives
	Managing in a Dynamic Environment
	Organizational Climate
	Competitive Analysis
	Diverse Workforce Workshop
	Advanced Program for Middle Managers
	Advanced Program for Directors
	Ethics and Values
Recent Speeches	"Succeeding in Corporate America"–1988
	"Networking in Corporate America"–1989
	"Managing a Diverse Workforce"–1989

Bibliography

This biliography is in two parts: Part 1 is an annotated periodicals listing, and Part 2 is a standard listing. Both parts are referenced in the body of this study.

Part 1—Periodicals

Asante, Molefi and Alice Davis. "Black and White Communication: Analyzing Work Place Encounters." *Journal of Black Studies* 16.1 (Sept. 1985):77–93.

> Their article demonstrates how situational modality converges with cultural modalities to create either understanding or misunderstanding in the work force among culturally dissimilar employees and employers.

Baron, Robert A. "Attributions and Organizational Conflict." *The Organization Behavior of Human Decision Processes* 41 (1988):111–127.

> This article explores situations where the individuals behave in a provocative, conflict inducing manner, often attributing such actions to external causes (e.g., "I'm only following orders"). In this article it is hypothesized that when such statements are perceived as accurate (sincere), they will mitigate negative reactions and reduce subsequent conflict. Various subjects were examined and as a result the subjects reported the most negative reactions under conditions where their

opponent falsely attributed his conflict reducing actions to external causes.

Cambridge, Charles B. "The Impact of Organization Theory and Affirmative Action On Organizational Behavior: Some Empirical Implications." *The Journal of Black Studies* 18.1 (Sept. 1987):97–104.

This article covers some of the implications of the impact of EEO/AA on organizations in American society. The author concludes after critique of certain studies on the same subject, that it will take time before we can adequately evaluate the response of work organizations in American society to EEO and AA requirements before we can properly assess how organizations are contributing to the upward mobility of racial minorities.

Darling, John R. and Raymond E. Taylor. "Upward Management: Getting In Step With the Boss." *Business* 37.2 (Apr.–June 1986):3–8.

This article identifies social style as a concept that can be used to manage upward more effectively. The authors point to the fact that organizational psychologists have identified four basic styles of relating to others, and the employee who knows these styles can use them to influence management. The four different kinds are: (1) the people person (amiable), (2) the thought people (analytical), (3) the action person (driver), and (4) the front person (expressive). The effective organization, they conclude, includes and values all four types of managers. They point out that the most productive management leadership team in a given organization will likely have a balance of individuals who reflect each of the four social styles.

Fenton, Stephen. "Explaining and Blaming: Racism and Sociology." *Patterns of Prejudice* 22.1 (1988):20–30.

This paper focuses on the psychological study of racism and race relations in particular, and sociology in general. The author explores an acute problem—the problem of distinguishing between attributing cause and assigning blame.

Field, Richard and David A. Vanseters. "Management By Expectations (MBE): The Power of Positive Prophesy." *Journal of General Management* 14.2 (Winter 1988):19–33.

This article introduces the new concept of management by expectations rather than management by objectives. The latter, they state, has proved very useful in providing organizational structure and planning direction for companies. The authors suggest, however, that the critical ingredient is to establish expectations because it transcends the other management approaches, since instead of focusing on the rationale and objective components management, it stresses the human component. They point out that excellent companies owe their resiliency and success not to their organizational structure or business administration skills, but to the magnitude of the positive expectations of their employees and customers.

Gamal, Irv and C. Woody McLaughlin. "Organizational Change: Blessing or Burden." *Personnel Administrator* (Aug. 1989):94–95.

This article points to issues that need better understanding when an organization embarks on change. The need to integrate detail planning, orientation, training systems, strong internal communications, and troubleshooting prior to implementation is stressed. The impact of change on employee attitude is emphasized and open communications are necessary to ensure support.

Hoffman, Eric. "Racial Difference In Supervisors' Attitudes Towards Coworkers." *Journal of Black Studies* 18.2 (Dec. 1987):139–161.

This paper focuses on the personality attributes in leadership. The author explores the differences in personality attributes between Black and White work supervisors.

Hylton, Richard D. "Working in America." *Black Enterprise* (Aug. 1988):63–66.

This article reports the poll results of Blacks' opinions on their jobs, careers, and aspirations. It points out that those polled were optimistic and dedicated to hard work, although widespread dissatisfaction was expressed about the opportunities available to Blacks in Corporate America.

Jans, N. A. "Organizational Commitment, Career Factors and Career/Life Stage." *Journal of Organizational Behavior* 10 (1989):249–266.

This study was to investigate organizational commitment in a career context. It addressed two main issues: first, when a person is pursuing a career in a particular organization, what are the factors associated with that career in that organization which affects organizational commitment, a commitment and its antecedents. It was shown that examination of the interplay of the independent variables across career life stages gives insight into the dynamics of organizational commitment.

Jacobson, Cardell K. "Resistance To Affirmative Action: Self Interest or Racism." *Journal of Conflict Resolution* 29.2 (June 1985):306–329.

This paper examines racial threat for self interest, new symbolic racism, and old fashioned racism as predictors of attitude about affirmative action programs.

Kinder, Donald R. "The Continuing American Dilemma: White Resistance To Racial Change Forty Years After Mydal." *Journal of Social Issues* 42.2 (1986):151–171.

This paper exposes the fact that after dramatic changes in public opinion and social custom over the past forty years, why do many White Americans continue to oppose efforts to bring about racial equality? The authors put forth two concepts that may explain the question. One is real intangible threats Whites may feel to their personal lives and the other is symbolic racism.

King, R. Sharon. "At the Cross Roads." *Black Enterprise* (Aug. 1988):45–54.

The article discusses Black women's progress in Corporate America and what accounts for it. Projections are made of the group in the work force population by the year 2000 and what positions and what companies are influencing this growth.

Murphy, Charles J. "The Invisibility of Black Workers In Organizational Behavior." *The Journal of Social and Behavioral Sciences* 19.3–4 (Spring–Fall 1973):1–12.

This article addresses itself to problems which Blacks and other minority group members might encounter while being employed by, managing or attempting to interface with an organization. The article points out that whatever roles Blacks may happen to assume in organizations, it would seem reasonable to expect different organizational behavior processes which are related to important organizational variables. It argues that although these racial differences and behavioral processes are and have been apparent to many Blacks, White organizational researchers have never sought to develop techniques, motivational processes, organizational policies, and practices which might have increased job satisfaction for Blacks, and perhaps over-all, organizational effectiveness.

Pettigrew, Thomas F. "Modern Racial Prejudice in America: Social Psychological Dimensions of Political Model-ing." *Patterns of Prejudice* 22.4 (1988):3–12.

This paper covers the current views of racial prejudice in America. It discusses how recent politicians mirror more accurately the modern racial style of White America. This style extends to all aspects of society. The author points to civil rights movements as being the key driving force for current White American thinking for a change.

Rasnic, Carroll E. "The Supreme Court And Affirmative Ac-tion: An Evolving Standard or Compounded Confusion?" *Employee Relations* LJY14 (Autumn 1988):175–190.

This paper summarizes eight different affirmative action cases and compares the various affirmative ac-tion programs involved in an effort to ascertain a developing standard and offer to employers guidance on how to apply the Court's various directives to their own situation.

Scarr, Sandra. "Race and Gender As Psychological Vari-ables." *American Psychologist* 43.1 (Jan. 1988):56–64.

The author argues that cowardice about minority and gender differences in research will lead us nowhere. She argues that more research should be done which highlight race and gender variables in order to inform us what we need to do to help under-represented people to succeed in this society. Her point is that we cannot afford to hide our heads for fear of socially un-comfortable discoveries.

Thompson, Kevin D. "Starting Over." *Black Enterprise* (Aug. 1988):58–61.

This article covers the changes occurring in strategies employed by professional women to increase their job status. More and more Black women are fleeing the corporate nest to spread their entrepreneurial wings. It is shown how networking among their peers has facilitated their efforts.

Weigel, Russell H. and Paul W. Howes. "Conceptions of Racial Prejudice: Symbolic Racism Reconsidered." *Journal of Social Issues* 41.3 (1985):117–138.

This paper provides an in-depth review of symbolic racism. The authors conclude that (a) the conceptual and empirical distinctions between symbolic racism and "oldfashioned" prejudice have been exaggerated and (b) symbolic racism may be best understood as one symptom of generalized tendencies to derogate out-groups.

Part 2—Books and periodicals

Alderfer, Clayton, Charleen Alderfer, Leota Tucker, and Robert Tucker. "Diagnosing Race Relations in Management." *Journal of Applied Behavioral Science* (1980):135–165.

Allport, Gordon W. *The Nature of Prejudice.* Reading, MA: Addison Wesley Publishing Co., Inc., 1979.

Anderson, Bernard E. *Moving Ahead: Black Managers In American Business.* New York, NY: McGraw-Hill, 1978.

Becker, Gary S. *The Economics of Discrimination.* 2nd ed. Chicago, IL: University of Chicago Press, 1957.

Bennett, Jr., Lerone. *Before the Mayflower: A History of Black America.* 6th ed. Chicago, IL: Johnson Publishing Co., 1987.

———. *The Challenge of Blackness.* Chicago, IL: Johnson Publishing Co., 1986.

————. *The Shaping of Black America*. Chicago, IL: Johnson Publishing Co., 1975.

Billingsley, Andrew. *Black Families in White America*. New York, NY: Simon and Schuster, 1968.

Bowser, Benjamin P. "Race Relations in the 1980's: The Case of the United States." *The Journal of Black Studies* 15.3 (1985):307–324.

Brown, Harold A. and David L. Ford, Jr. "An Exploratory Analysis of Discrimination in the Employment of Black MBA Graduates." *Journal of Applied Psychology* 62.1 (1977):50–56.

Campbell, Angus. *White Attitudes Toward Black People*. Ann Arbor, MI: Institute for Social Research, 1971.

Cravens, David W., Gerald E. Hills, and Robert B. Woodruff. Marketing *Decision Making: Concepts and Strategies*. Homewood, IL: Richard D. Irwin, 1976.

Davis, George and Glegg Watson. *Black Life in Corporate America: Swimming in the Mainstream*. Garden City, NY: Anchor Press, 1985.

Dickens, Jr., Floyd and Jacqueline B. Dickens. *The Black Manager: Making It In The Corporate World*. New York, NY: AMACOM, 1984.

Eitzen, D. Stanley and Maxine Baca-Zinn. *Social Problems*. Needham, MA: Allyn and Bacon, 1989.

Farley, Reynolds. *Black and Whites: Narrowing the Gap?* Cambridge, MA: Harvard University Press, 1984.

Fernandez, John P. *Black Managers In White Corporations*. New York, NY: John Wiley and Sons, 1975.

Germann, Richard, Diane Blumenson, and Peter Arnold. *Working and Liking It*. New York, NY: Ballantine Books, 1984.

Hernton, Calvin C. *Sex and Racism in America*. New York, NY: Grove Press, 1965.

Johnston, William B. and Arnold H. Packer. *Workforce 2000: Work and Workers for the 21st Century.* Washington, D.C.: Hudson Institute, Inc., 1987.

Jones, Jr., Edward W. "What's It Like To Be A Black Manager." *Corporate Business Review On Management* (July–Aug. 1973):102–110.

Jones, Reginald L., ed. *The Black Psychology.* New York, NY: Harper and Row, 1980.

Kinder, Donald R. "The Continuing American Dilemma: White Resistance To Racial Change Forty Years After Mydal." *Journal of Social Issues* 42.2 (1986):151–171.

Kochman, Thomas. *Black and White Styles in Conflict.* Chicago, IL: University of Chicago Press, 1981.

Montagu, Ashley, ed. *Race and I.Q.* New York, NY: Oxford University Press, 1975.

Murphy, Charles J. "The Invisibility of Black Workers In Organizational Behavior." *The Journal of Social and Behavioral Sciences* 19.3–4 (Spring–Fall 1973):1–12.

Nixon, Regina. *Black Managers in Corporate America: Alienation or Integration?* Washington, D.C.: National Urban League, 1980.

Schuman, Howard, Charlotte Steeh, and Lawrence Bobo. *Racial Attitudes in America: Trends and Interpretations.* Cambridge, MA: Harvard University Press, 1985.

Schulke, Flip, ed. *Martin Luther King, Jr.* New York, NY: W. W. Norton, 1976.

Schiller, Bradley R. *The Economics of Property and Discrimination.* Englewood Cliffs, NJ: Prentice-Hall, 1984.

Semyonov, Moshe, Danny R. Hoyt, and Richard I. Scott. "Place, Race, and Differential Occupational Opportunity." *Demography.* 21.2 (May 1984).

Sitkoff, Harvard. *The Struggle for Black Equality 1954 through 1980.* New York, NY: Hill and Wang, 1981.

Sniderman, Paul M., Survey Research Center, and Michael G. Hagen. *Race and Inequality*. Chatham, NJ: Chatham House, 1985.

Thurow, Lester C. *Poverty and Discrimination*. Washington, D.C.: Brookings Institution, 1969.

Triandis, Harry C., ed. *Variations in Black and White Perceptions of the Social Environment*. Chicago, IL: University of Illinois Press, 1976.

Wells, Jr., Leroy and Carl L. Jennings. "Black career advancement and white reactions: Remnants of 'Herrenvolk' democracy and the scandalous paradox." *NTL Sunrise Seminars* I (1984):41–47.

Wilhelm, Sidney M. "Black/White Equality: The Socioeconomic Conditions of Blacks in America Part II." *The Journal of Black Studies* 14.2 (Dec. 1983):151–184.

Wilson, William Julius. *The Declining Significant of Race: Blacks and Changing American Institution*. 2nd ed. Chicago, IL: University of Chicago Press, 1980.

Work, John W. *Race, Economics, and Corporate America*. Wilmington, DE: Scholarly Resources, Inc., 1984.

Contributor

Margaret B. Miller-Vaughan is research associate and professor of graduate management programs at St. Thomas University in the Twin Cities area, serving also on the Task Force for Business Ethics. She is a member of the Core Faculty in Administration/Management of the Ph.D. programs at Walden University of Minneapolis. In the course of her work she has done extensive traveling in Europe, Asia, and Latin America. Her research and consulting range across disciplines and industrial sectors. Her relationship to the author grew from renewed interests in innovative methods to use in advanced education levels for American business people. She holds a doctorate in international business and human capital investment from the University of Iowa, earned in 1981. She is president of Miller and Associates, a consulting group.